Book Bait

Detailed Notes on Adult Books
Popular with Young People

FOURTH EDITION

Compiled by
ELINOR WALKER

AMERICAN LIBRARY ASSOCIATION
Chicago and London 1988

Elinor Walker has worked with young people for more than 50 years as a teacher, young adult librarian, reviewer of young adult books, and as coordinator of young adult services at the Carnegie Library of Pittsburgh for more than 25 years. Walker is the author of the three previous editions of *Book Bait* (ALA, 1957, 1967, 1979) and of *Doors to More Mature Reading* (ALA, 1964, 1981).

Illustration by Mary Phelan

Composed by Compositors
    in Caledonia

Printed on 50-pound Booktext natural,
    a pH-neutral stock, and
    bound in 10-point Carolina
    cover stock by
    Bookcrafters
    ∞

Library of Congress Cataloging-in-Publication Data

Book bait.

    Includes index.
    1. Youth—Books and reading. 2. Young adult literature—Stories, plots, etc. 3. Libraries, Young people's—Book lists. 4. Junior high school libraries—Book lists. 5. High school libraries—Book lists. I. Walker, Elinor.
    Z1037.B7216   1988   028.1'625055   88-987
    [PN1009.A1]
    ISBN 0-8389-0491-2

Contents

Preface   v

Book Bait   1

Subject Index of Main Entries   156

Title Index   161

Preface

The titles included in Book Bait are adult books heartily recommended by young people who have read them. The majority of the books are important because they are remembered with pleasure and many times contribute to the growth and development of young readers. Often teens will return a book and request "another just like this one." In these books, young people have discovered new interests to pursue further. The books offer lessons in brotherhood, patience, persistence, love, courage, and understanding that will enable readers to face their own problems with the determination to solve them. Books like these can open a whole new world of enjoyment in reading.

Good junior high readers today are much more sophisticated and mature in their thinking than they were when I first began to work with them years ago. Television and movies have had a lot to do with this change. In order that this fourth edition would reflect the opinions of today's teenagers, I worked closely with a group of seventh, eighth, and ninth graders. We met every week the year around, and they read the books I gathered for them. They also suggested ones that they had discovered, and I added those for the group to read and discuss at our meetings. In selecting books for the group, I found that many of the easier adult books either were poorly conceived or included controversial elements. The young people were not concerned by the inclusion of bedroom scenes and were surprised at first when I objected to a lot of detail. However, they acknowledged that all younger teenagers were not as sophisticated as they were, and they said they were becoming bored with that kind of detail. I found that I had to choose more mature books than I had for previous editions, and the young readers had no difficulty with most.

Several of the boys were science fiction fans, and on their urging, some of the girls read the books they recommended. These boys would read other types of books if a reviewer had been really enthusiastic. I found that adventure, mystery, science fiction, family stories (both modern and of older times), true stories of the disabled, fantasies, intrigues, true stories of German concentration camps, love stories, World War II and Vietnam War experiences, and adult books with some teenage characters were the most popular. None of the young people showed an interest in problem stories written for teens. These young people were good readers and spoke their minds freely. If several of them turned thumbs down on a book, we no longer considered it. These young people also selected the titles to be retained from the third edition of *Book Bait*.

You may be interested in the reasons the young readers gave for voting against books: they disliked books they saw as poorly written; slow moving; whose characters were just names—not well developed; having far too much violence; or unrealistic. A major complaint, of course, was "I couldn't get interested in the book."

Young adult librarians across the United States were consulted and asked to give their opinions of books to be considered for the new edition. One told me that her library was buying fewer adult books for young adult collections, and this is probably true in other cities, judging from the smaller number of books they recommended. Some publishers today seem no longer interested in issuing adult books that can be highly recommended and purchased for teenage readers. On the other hand, some paperback publishers have flooded the market with poorly written, badly conceived stories that do nothing to motivate young people to increase their reading interest or ability. Some librarians are buying these by the dozens instead of demanding better, more mature books from the publishers. One reason is, of course, the high price of hardbound books today. Librarians and teachers should get together with the publishers. You would certainly buy good paperbacks in preference to the poor ones if you could get them. You are hurting your readers now, and they have little chance of developing into good lifetime adult readers unless you help.

Many libraries have a section in their children's room labeled "Teen" or "Young Adult." However, the adult books of interest to and suitable for these older children are put on adult shelves and are not easily found. Unless a library has a staff person who is interested in teenagers and who knows the adult collection and what to recommend to teens, young people are neglected and discouraged. In a library I visited recently, I began to talk with a young teen who was browsing unsuccessfully along the shelves, and she finally said, "I can't find anything here [in the children's room], and I don't know where to look in there [the adult department]."

There is real concern in the United States today about the poor education that children and young people are receiving in the schools. Librarians have to share the responsibility for this situation. Most children's librarians do a good job, their patrons are encouraged to read, and they learn to love books. Students in junior highs, middle schools, and senior highs need knowledgeable librarians who can motivate students to continue reading. To do so these librarians need good books they can recommend wholeheartedly. Public library budget cuts have eliminated many positions for librarians to work exclusively with teens, placing more responsibility on those working with adults. Book Bait should have very good use with these librarians. Why do a terrific job with children and then drop them when they should be getting an enthusiastic reception in adult departments?

The books in Book Bait were selected for the best readers in seventh, eighth, and ninth grades. These books should be stepping-stones to more mature books that young people will read in senior high. They should also be recommended to average readers in senior high. Care has been taken to choose books with a minimum of objectionable language and scenes, and where these elements occur, they have probably been pointed out.

The main entry has a long annotation that summarizes the book's content and attempts to give its flavor. The second paragraph lists the best features of the book and comments on its appeal to teens. This paragraph is in no way meant to be a review of the book. The third paragraph gives suggestions for booktalks. Many librarians I know do not like to give book-talks, and they say they don't have time to read. To save time for new librarians, Book Bait has always listed pages where there is an episode that can be used for a booktalk. Often that is all the librarian must read. Nothing can be more satisfying than to see the enthusiasm of young people checking books out when the librarian has finished a booktalk. One can be presented in a history, social science, or science class as well as an English class. I once worked with a librarian who spoke in French classes. It is fun. Try it!

The final paragraph briefly describes additional carefully selected books that one can suggest to those readers who are enthusiastic about the main entry and want a similar book. In some cases a juvenile title that might lead to the main entry has been included. An asterisk (∘) is placed after follow-up titles that are also main entries, indicating that long annotations may be found elsewhere in the compilation. The book has a subject index of main entries and a title index.

I want to thank the following librarians and members of their staffs for advice in compiling this new edition:

Penny Jeffrey, Cleveland, Ohio
Elizabeth Keen, Philadelphia, Pennsylvania
Lydia LaFleur, New York, New York
Linda Lapides, Baltimore, Maryland
Susan B. Madden, Seattle, Washington
Hazel Rochman, Chicago, Illinois
Christy Tyson, Spokane, Washington
Jackie Woody, Glenarden, Maryland

Barbara J. Duree and Sally Estes of *Booklist* were also very helpful. Sally, working as the consulting editor on the final manuscript, revised annotations for optimal clarity of subject matter and plot. She also suggested titles for inclusion.

I am greatly indebted for the assistance of the staffs of the Edina and St. Louis Park libraries, which are branches of the Hennepin County Library System in suburban Minneapolis. New on the staff of the St. Louis Park Library, Pamela Holt did not yet know the young people who used the library or the junior high school librarians. As a result of her talking at county staff meetings about my need to work with young readers, Bill Erickson, then children's librarian at Edina, contacted the junior high school librarians in the area, and Treffle Daniels arranged for me to speak to a group of students at his junior high school. Librarian Nancy Bales also sent a student from her school. A sign posted in the Edina Library brought in readers from private and outlying schools to join us. The following seventh, eighth, and ninth graders worked with me; they are good students and in many activities at school, at church, with their families, and in the community: Lisa Brinkman, Michelle Chang, Kim Christian, Karen Kiang, Mia Lushine, Karen Mattison, Derek Mogck, Julie Mueller, Brett Pertuz, Laurie Peterson, Sean Salene, Laura South, and John Workinger. David Addington and Sara Lewis were with me from the beginning and missed very few meetings. Both are avid and discriminating readers and made an especially valuable contribution.

I am also grateful to the staff of the Public Library in Cresco, Iowa, for obtaining for me many of the books published in late 1986 and in 1987. Without their assistance I could not have completed the work on Book Bait.

Book Bait

Auel, Jean N.

The Clan of the Cave Bear.   1980.   Crown.

In a novel set in prehistoric times, a five-year-old girl playing on a river bank in the early morning is left alone when an earthquake suddenly topples the lean-to and her family into a huge crack in the earth. Days later she is found unconscious by a small Neanderthal clan searching for a new cave. The child is taken up by the medicine woman, Iza, whose wise but crippled brother Creb, the most powerful man in the clan, manages to learn the girl's name, which sounds like Ayla. The clan soon finds a fine cave, and when Brun, the clan leader, wants to abandon Ayla, Creb saves her by claiming that they have found the cave only because of her. Since each clan member has a totem, Creb ponders before he judges the cave bear to be best for Ayla. The day before the ceremony of the totems, Brun's son Broud, the center of attention for making his first kill as a hunter, is angry and jealous of Ayla's strong totem, feeling that she has stolen some of his glory, and from then on he dislikes her. Iza takes Ayla with her as she searches for food and medicinal plants, teaching the girl to help. In time Ayla, now a young woman, goes out searching alone, and one day she secretly watches a young boy being trained in the use of a sling. Afterward she picks up an old sling and with practice becomes very adept, experimenting until she can fire two stones quickly, one after another—something she knows the hunters cannot do. Because the fate of any woman who touches a weapon is death, she keeps her new skill a secret until one fall she has to use her sling to save Broud's small son, Brac. In spite of this, Broud condemns her, but Creb and Brun find a way to save her life. Before Iza dies she tells the young woman that when Broud succeeds his father, she will have to leave the clan, and she does.

The articulate, blue-eyed, blond Ayla, presumably of Cro-Magnon hominid stock, stands in sharp contrast to her adoptive Neanderthal tribe in this very long and detailed but extremely interesting novel with well-drawn main characters. The book is highly recommended by young adult librarians across the country, and my readers were enthusiastic about it. There are some sexual references: in description of the animal-like sex act practiced by the clan, and in Ayla's uneasy relationship with Broud: after she becomes a woman, and he learns how much she hates to submit to him, he often insists on sex wherever they are. However, there is a significant difference between reading about early man's brief sex act and the detailed erotic descriptions found in the sequels to *Clan of the Cave Bear.*

A booktalk can be built on the finding of Ayla, the discovery of a new cave home, and Creb's decision to take Iza and Ayla to his own hearth, pages 10–15, 20–23, 44–46, 48, 51–55.

Thomas Millstead's first book, *Cave of the Moving Shadows,* tells of the exciting adventures of a twelve-year-old boy, a member of a Cro-Magnon tribe. Young people who enjoyed this book can be introduced to *The Clan of the Cave Bear. National Geographic* for November, 1985, provides a good introduction to factual information about prehistoric discoveries. *Lucy: The Beginning of Humankind°* by Donald Johanson and Maitland Edey can be suggested as a follow-up. John Reader, who became interested in fossils while working as a photojournalist for *Life, Time,* and *National Geographic,* has written in *Missing Links* about the skeletal remnants of ancient man unearthed over the years. His history is arranged chronologically by the names assigned to each discovery—Neanderthal, Java, etc.—and is enhanced by fine color photographs. Although many more discoveries have been made since *The Neanderthals* by George Constable was published, young people will find this nonfiction account of early man fascinating reading. Bjorn Kurten, one of Europe's leading paleontologists, has written several novels about the ice age. In *Singletusk* he tells of Tiger, one of the first *Homo sapiens*, who had to send his son Whitespear to find a great healer. Most of the book tells of Whitespear's adventures as he carries out his assignment.

Benchley, Peter

Girl of the Sea of Cortez. 1982. Doubleday.

Sixteen-year-old Paloma lives with her mother, Miranda, and her younger brother, Jo, on the island of Santa Maria. Two years earlier Paloma's father, Jobim, had drowned in a terrible *chubasco*, but he had fostered her love of the sea by teaching her many things about it and its creatures when they were diving together; Jo, however, is afraid of the sea. After Jobim's death, Paloma goes alone to a seamount her father had discovered—a place where deep-water currents flow along the seafloor, strike the seamount, and create an upwelling that carries plankton and tiny shrimp upward, drawing fish to the area to feed. Fish, the island's main source of income, have become less plentiful because of poor fishing methods, and the fishermen have not found the seamount, which is about an hour's paddle from Paloma's home. While diving there one day she discovers an immense manta ray lying absolutely still above the seamount. Diving near it, she sees a deep wound near its left "horn," from which dangle ropes, and she surmises it had battled its way out of a fisherman's net. On her next dive she grabs and yanks a handful of rope, and the manta takes off, tumbling her into a spinning somersault. When she tells Jo and her mother about it that night, Jo does not believe her. Finding the manta again the next day, she is able to get all the rope out and cut away the putrescent flesh. Surfacing, she is confronted by Jo and his friends, who immediately realize what a rich find the seamount is. When Paloma climbs into her pirogue and heads for home, Jo, who has a nasty temper, capsizes her boat, punches a hole in it, and takes off for home. Paloma's experience, before she finally reaches home late that night, is a terrifying trial and one of the high points of the story. She is heartsick when the boys come home with a tremendous load of fish from the seamount, and she follows them on their next fishing trip. The final episode concerns the manta and its revenge on the boys.

Anyone who is fascinated by the sea and diving will be intrigued by the story and will learn a great deal quite painlessly. The best-drawn character is Jobim, who is vitalized mainly through Paloma's recollections of him.

A good scene for booktalking is Paloma's finding a pearl in an oyster to add to the collection her father had started. He had wanted to give Miranda a natural pearl necklace for their twentieth wedding anniversary, pages 44–50. One of Paloma's first encounters with the manta will also make a good book-talk, pages 51–66.

It is a joy to read *Dolphins*, in which Jacques-Yves Cousteau and Phillippe Diole describe their adventures and experiments with dolphins. The book is enhanced by beautiful color photographs. In *Secret Languages of the Sea*, Robert F. Burgess has packed fascinating facts and experiments with sharks, whales, and especially dolphins. He also records the intelligence of ordinary fish, demonstrated in one incident when fish showed divers where sea urchins were hiding so that the men would dig the urchins out and feed them to the waiting fish. In *The Man Who Rode the Sharks*, Williams R. Royal describes his first experience in diving, when he was stationed as a civil engineer on a small South Pacific island. Also try recommending, as a follow-up, Pierre Boulle's *The Whale of the Victoria Cross*,° in which a female whale gratefully adopts the British warship that saved her from killer whales. A young reader may want to try diving after reading *Girl of the Sea of Cortez*, and *Exploring Underwater* by John Culleney and Edward Crocket offers a detailed explanation of everything a diver needs to know, from the purchase of equipment to the undersea of the future. In *Aka*, Tristan Jones has combined the dolphins' attraction to the human race with the fate of a man who was pulled overboard by a giant turtle he had caught while on a single-handed around-the-world race. Some explicit love scenes in the beginning chapters may limit this to more mature readers.

Boardman, Peter

The Shining Mountain. 1982. Dutton.

Peter Boardman began climbing at an early age, and by the time he is in his early twenties he has established such a fine record that noted climber Chris Bonington offers him the opportunity to join an expedition to the southwest face of Everest; Peter was one of the four who reached the summit. Back at his demanding job as a national officer of the British Mountaineering Council, Peter is tired and depressed, especially after hearing that Joe Tasker and Dick Renshaw have climbed Dunagiri with no backup team. Later in the year, Joe Tasker suggests that he and Pete climb the supposedly unclimbable west face of Changabang. Here Pete tells of training in the freezer of a frozen-food plant, the journey out of India, the purchase of supplies, and the trip up to base camp by train and bus and on foot. Their Indian liaison officer, whom they were required to take along, refuses to stay alone at base camp and leaves with the porters who carried their gear. It takes them from September 4 to October 15 to push their way up the seemingly impossible terrain to the summit. The reader feels almost as exhausted and certainly more tense than the climbers while reading of the obstacles they face and overcome. Winter is upon them, and they have to make the difficult descent as quickly as possible. When they finally reach base camp, they find there a party of Italian climbers and an American woman, the only survivor of a group that was climbing the nearby Dunagiri. Pete and Joe go with two porters to find the bodies and bury them in a crevasse near where the climbers ended their fall. Their conquering of the west face has been acknowledged by mountain climbers as the most remarkable accomplishment ever achieved in the Himalayas.

This is a good book to use for introducing readers to mountain climbing. It is an account uncomplicated by the activities of a large group of climbers and base camp personnel. There is a glossary of climbing terms, which the readers should be encouraged to use. Boardman writes well, including enough detail to demonstrate the difficulties of the climb, the weather, and the lack of oxygen.

Beginning at the bottom of page 55 and reading the next ten pages, the booktalker can find plenty of interesting facts as the two young men begin their real climbing. At the bottom of page 73 and on page 74 an exciting few moments are described.

In *Savage Arena* Joe Tasker, who had been Pete Boardman's climbing companion, wrote of that ascent as well as his climb on the Eiger in Switzerland and on Dunagiri, K-2, and

Kangchanjunga in the Himalayas. His accounts are dramatic, vividly descriptive and personal. He and Pete died on a push to the summit of Everest in 1982. Arthur Roth's *Eiger: Wall of Death* is a history of climbers who attempted to or did climb the Eiger, particularly the concave north wall, which was labeled impossible for years. Although well done, it may not have the appeal of the first-hand accounts. *Tiger of the Snows* by Tenzing Norgay, if available, is a good book to use in introducing readers to climbs by large teams. Chris Bonington has written several good books on his climbing experiences, but his are for the more experienced reader, as he included background information about raising funds, assembling a team and equipment, and organizing the camps and climbing teams. In *The Challenge*, Reinhold Messner tells of the failure of the Italian Lhotse South Face Expedition (of which he was a member) to reach the summit because of extremely bad weather and avalanches.

Boulle, Pierre

The Whale of the Victoria Cross.   1983.   Vanguard.

When the British fleet is on its long voyage from England to the Falkland Islands, the five thousand or so men on the transports are bored. One day the destroyer *Daring* picks up on radar a black spot dead ahead, moving slowly within range. Is it a whale or a submarine? The alarm sounds, and the men dash to battle stations, while the captain sends for Bjorg, a Falklander and former whaler, who knows more about whales than Captain Clark wants to know. This is the first hint that the story may be amusing. Bjorg is not sure what it is at first, but the spot suddenly changes direction and depth, coming toward the *Daring*, and Bjorg sees two blue whales, a male and female swimming side by side. Then a new object appears on radar—a triangular sail moving at tremendous speed: a killer whale! The blue whales take off, but the killer is faster. Soon many triangular sails are seen, and the men watch the killers attack and kill the male. The female sounds and in a few minutes comes up close to the *Daring* as if asking for help. The killers turn their attention to the female. Should the ship use its guns to protect the female? The captain has thirty seconds to make up his mind; risking the end of his career in the Navy, he

6

shouts "Fire!" The guns open up while the men roar their approval. When the admiral wants to know what is going on, there is no reply until a subordinate says the captain is too busy but not to worry. An unheard-of response! This is only the beginning of an outlandish but really amusing story of the whale the sailors called Auntie Margot. She repays the fleet for her protection in more ways then one.

It is pleasing to see this fine author let himself go with a far-out idea in a story peopled with a wide array of characters, from an officious admiral to the lowliest seaman, all of whom make for entertaining reading. Several of my ninth graders enjoyed this book.

A booktalk would have to tell about the radar discovering a bleep that turns out to be blue whales instead of an enemy submarine and should probably include the rescue of the female. There is a good deal of conversation in these pages, so the reading goes quickly, pages 24–37, 45–59.

Suggest R. L. Fisher's *The Prince of Whales*, a fantasy about a whale named Toby who wants to learn to sing. Eventually Toby's magnificent voice and courage convince humankind to stop its carnage against endangered species. *Sounding* by Hank Searles is a different type of story concerned with the relationship of humans and whales. One facet of the book deals with the lives of a pod of sperm whales, while the other tells of the sonar officer on a disabled Russian submarine resting on a high ridge deep in the ocean. Shot from a torpedo tube, the officer is saved by an old sperm whale. Anyone with a real interest in whales and dolphins should be introduced to *So Remorseless a Havoc* by Robert McNally, who discusses the physiology of the cetaceans, the history of the whaling industry, the concern of people in the United States for the survival of whales and dolphins, and whales and dolphins in legend and literature.

Bradley, Marian Zimmer

The House between the Worlds.   1980.   Doubleday.

Agreeing to help Dr. Lewis Garnoch, a professor of parapsychology, test a new drug that is supposed to enhance extrasensory powers, Cameron Fenton is injected with the drug. Leaving his body behind, he walks through a wall and out of the laboratory building. He finds himself in an alternate world watching a battle between the defenders of the Faerie Queen, Kerridis, and a mass of knife-wielding, ugly, hairy beings, who finally carry off the queen and her companion, Irielle. Through Fenton, who follows them, the people of Alfar are able to rescue their women, but Fenton's time as a 'tweenman in the other world is limited because the drug is wearing off, and he returns to his body on the Berkeley campus. Though his experience seems very real to him, Garnoch's assistant Sally, who debriefs him, considers his adventure a dream. On his second trip, Fenton is captured by Pentarn, leader of yet another world, who asks Fenton to work for him because the two look much alike. However, once again Fenton must return to his body. Though Garnoch refuses him a third injection, Fenton is able to buy some of the drug in pill form on the street. After long thought, he takes a pill, and this time he arrives in unfamiliar territory where he sees the ironfolk, who had earlier captured Kerridis, pouring out of a cave. Just in time, he hears a voice say, "Quick, in here," and another cave mouth opens and then closes behind him. Inside he finds a gnome who helps him get to Alfar, where he accomplishes little before returning to his body. Later Fenton demands that Garnoch restore to him the talisman he had brought back from his second journey to Alfar, but when the two men go to a print shop, which they have learned has a doorway to the other worlds, they grapple for the talisman just as they are translated—Garnoch to Alfar and Fenton to Pentarn's world. Pentarn offers Fenton a bracelet that will enable him to go between worlds in return for working for him, but a band of ironmen bursts in suddenly, and Fenton makes his escape with the bracelet as Pentarn and the ironfolk are killed by Alfar warriors.

The story is long, detailed, and very well written. There are a number of well-drawn, interesting characters. My science fiction fans highly recommended the book.

Fenton's first visit to Alfar is too long and detailed for a booktalk, but a talk could include Fenton's first reaction to the drug and go on to the first time he saw Kerridis, pages 6–16.

In Barbara Hambly's *The Time of the Dark*, also a story of travel between worlds, a young woman Ph.D. candidate helps an old wizard from another world and in doing so is forced at one point to visit his world, where many strange adventures await them. Intergalactic activity and possible war between other worlds and earth is the premise of *Way Station* by Clifford Simak. Enoch Wallace (124 years old but looking 30), keeper of a house used by galaxy inhabitants traveling the universe, is suspected of unlawful activity by U.S. Intelligence. In Gordon R. Dickson's *The Dragon and the George*, college assistants Jim Eckert and Angie Farrell are transported to another world, where she is held captive and he finds himself in the body of a dragon. The story concerns Angie's rescue.

Bradshaw, Gillian

The Beacon at Alexandria.   1986.   Houghton Mifflin.

Charis, only daughter of well-to-do Theodoros of Ephesus, is encouraged to read Hippocrates because her tutor admires his beautiful writing. Charis, however, is pleased because of her interest in medicine; she can practice what she learns on injured songbirds and lapdogs. When she is fifteen, the new governor, Festinus, comes to investigate her father, who has done no wrong but is terrified of the man. Charis and her brother Thorion are introduced to the governor, a widower. Shortly Festinus decides to marry Charis, and her father consents. Unable to avoid the marriage, Charis decides to disguise herself as a eunuch and go to Alexandria to study medicine. Thorion reserves space in a ship, pays half the fare, and provides an appropriate second-hand wardrobe. Her maid cuts her hair and shows her how to properly arrange a man's clothing. Instead of being married on the first of May, she lands in Alexandria. The author tells of her finding a doctor who will accept a eunuch as an assistant, of her attending lectures at the museum, and of her gradually making friends with and winning the admiration of some of the male students. The city is in political and religious turmoil, and riots are always threatening. Fortunately, Chariton, as she is now called, makes several valuable friends because of her skill in treating patients. Near the end of her training, when violence erupts, one of these friends sends her to Thrace, on the border between Roman-held territory and the Goths and Huns, to become head of a military hospital for Roman soldiers. She often travels several days from the hospital to care for important patients.

Two leaders in the area, Athanaric and Sebastianus, become her good friends. She respects both, but she loves Athanaric. Eventually she is captured by the Goths and has to treat their ill and wounded. Amalberga, wife of a Gothic leader, suspects that Chariton is a woman, and when questioned the girl has to confess that she is. She is sent to the women's quarters, and there is no way she can escape, although she still treats patients. Finally Athanaric manages to rescue her. By then he knows she is a woman and that he loves her.

This is a long book containing considerable history of the latter days of the Roman Empire, between 371 and 374 A.D. Charis is such an interesting, daring, and appealing character that the reader *must* find out what happens to her. The book is very well written and gives an excellent picture of the times.

For a booktalk use pages 13–47, which introduce Charis and her brother, her father, and Festinus and relate Charis's plan to escape to Alexandria. Or summarize the above and tell of Charis's first days in Alexandria, her problems, and her finding a doctor for whom she can work, pages 59–67.

For follow-ups, suggest the following. Although Lygia, a lovely Christian girl, and the young man, Vinicius, who loves her, are important in *Quo Vadis* by Henryk Sienkiewicz, it is Nero with his excesses who is the main character. The Apostle Peter and Paul of Tarsus meet death along with hundreds of Christians in this vividly described account. Really good readers should be encouraged to read *The Last Days of Pompeii* by Edward Bulwer-Lytton. In the months before the destruction of the city of Vesuvius in 78 A.D., Glaucus, a wealthy young Athenian, falls in love with Ione, a lovely Greek girl, and they plan to marry. This is opposed by Arbaces, a fabulously wealthy Egyptian and the girl's teacher and advisor, who decides to marry Ione himself. He might have been successful but for a blind slave girl. *The Darkness and the Dawn* by Thomas Costain takes place about seventy-five years later than *The Beacon at Alexandria* and is partly concerned with Attila and his attempt to conquer Rome. The main character is Nicolan, a boy sold as a slave to a master in Rome. As a young adult he succeeded in escaping and became a member of Attila's staff. Many obstacles stood in the way of the marriage of Nicolan and the exquisite Ildico, but they triumphed in the end.

Breuer, William B.

Devil Boats: The PT War against Japan. 1987. Presidio.

About 1927 Japanese generals and admirals began to plan an attack on the United States and Australia. These two nations had the greatest number of white people in the Pacific, and Japan expected to dominate the Pacific by taking over the Philippines and Australia and driving whites from the area. They start with the destruction of U.S. Navy ships at Pearl Harbor. Because the United States is totally unprepared for war, the Japanese have relatively little trouble taking the Philippines, and if it were not for two decrepit PT boats, General MacArthur and his staff would be captured. Despite the fact that the boats do not carry equipment for a long sea voyage and that they leave too abruptly to allow time for an overhaul of their engines, they make their way to Mindanao, where planes are to take the general to Australia. The PTs prove their value, and MacArthur recognizes their possibilities. He recommends his boat's captain, John Buckeley, for a Medal of Honor. This gives the skipper a chance to brief President Roosevelt and military leaders in Washington about events in the Philippines and the value of the PTs. Then Buckeley gives them MacArthur's order for the delivery of 200 PT boats in eight months' time, to be used in the destruction of Japanese transports. The enemy has taken possession of most of the important islands north of Australia. Japanese bombers are active over the continent, and Japan is building up supplies and armed forces for an invasion. The PT boats are equipped with torpedoes, depth charges, and guns, some using incendiary bullets. The author describes the actions of individual boats as they sank barges and ships loaded with food, ammunition, soldiers, and supplies. The slaughter of men on both sides is horrendous. Gradually MacArthur, using leapfrog tactics, returns to the Philippines. Not long after this, two atomic bombs end the war, but it is a bitter, bloody fight every inch of the way.

For anyone who likes war stories, this is an exciting, fascinating book detailing over three years of World War II in the Pacific. Men who fought in the PT boats provided the author with accounts of their experiences and with photographs.

11

Often it seemed impossible for the boats to escape after a devastating attack, but, as if by a miracle, many of them did.

For a booktalk, there are any number of events that could be used: the rescue of Lt. John F. Kennedy and his crew when their boat was sunk, pages 106–11; the rescue of an American pilot in a small bay surrounded by Japanese batteries, pages 174–78; and several short incidents when PTs attempted to stop the *Tokyo Express*, pages 94–97.

If the reader is interested also in submarine warfare, Edwin P. Hoyt's *Bowfin: The Story of One of America's Fabled Fleet Submarines* can be recommended. *Bowfin*, stationed in the Pacific during World War II, sinks 176,000 tons of Japanese ships on nine patrols. In *A Sailor's War*, Sam Bombard-Hobson tells of his training at the Royal Naval College, his assignment as a cadet on the flagship, *Queen Elizabeth*, and his experiences during World War II as second-in-command and, later, as captain of several destroyers. He has a wonderful sense of humor, humility, and great courage. Douglas Reeman's novel *A Ship Must Die* is the story of HMS *Andromeda*, which has been fighting in the Mediterranean but is finally sent to Australia to protect convoys against a German raider. *The Amindra Gamble* by John Sherlock and David Westheimer tells of British gold being sent to Canada on the same ship as thirty-seven English schoolboys, ages eight to thirteen, and their two chaperones. Enemy submarines are not the only danger threatening the ship. For readers also interested in World War II from the German viewpoint, suggest *U-Boat Commander* by Peter Cremer, one of the top German submarine commanders. In *The Cruelest Night*, Christopher Dobson, John Miller, and Ronald Payne reveal the tremendous loss of lives when refugees fleeing from eastern Germany ahead of the invading Russians are on ships sunk by Russian submarines in the Baltic Sea.

Bronte, Charlotte

Jane Eyre. 1847.

Jane, an orphan unwanted in her uncles' home, finds a dear friend and a career when she is sent to a private school. Upon finishing her education, she accepts a teaching position in a school and stays until the friend marries and leaves. Jane then looks for another place and eventually goes to

Thornfield Hall as governess to the owner's ward. That man, Mr. Rochester, has seldom stayed at his home for any length of time, but after he meets Jane, he finds a new attractiveness about the place. Several mysterious events, including a fire in the master's room, make Jane suspect there is something strange about the house, but the housekeeper and Mr. Rochester manage to quiet her fears and still her suspicions. She does not discover what is wrong until after her employer has asked her to marry him and she has accepted him. Their wedding ceremony is stopped by a man who claims to be the brother of Mr. Rochester's first wife. That poor woman is mad, still living, and confined to the third floor of Thornfield Hall. After this disclosure, Jane leaves Thornfield. The insane wife finally manages to set fire to the house and perishes in the flames. In trying to save her, Mr. Rochester loses one hand and his eyesight. Later, circumstances bring Jane and Mr. Rochester together again.

The mystery and excitement in unraveling the secret of Mr. Rochester's past, the fine, strong character of Jane, and the love story makes this a very enjoyable book.

For booktalks, use the incident of the fire in Mr. Rochester's room, which may be found near the end of chapter 15. The fact that the story begins slowly might be mentioned, as the first few chapters have discouraged some readers.

The teacher or librarian may want to prepare young readers for *Jane Eyre* by introducing them to *A London Season* by Anthea Bell. It is a romping novel of a lovely girl in her first season in London high society and her companion, a former governess. A scoundrel fails in his attempt to ruin the reputations of both young ladies, and both find their true loves. Also suggest *Rebecca*° by Daphne DuMaurier. Follow with *Wuthering Heights* by Charlotte Bronte's sister Emily. In this story, Heathcliffe had been a poor orphan as a child, and his resentment, bitterness, and pride make him want to get even with the family that had adopted him and with their neighbors for looking down on him. Those who have read both *Jane Eyre* and *Wuthering Heights* can be introduced to *Dark Quarter: The Story of the Brontes* and its sequel, *Path to a Silent Country* by Lynne Reed Banks. These books make the Bronte family come to life and give additional meaning to their writings.

Brown, Dee

Killdeer Mountain. 1983. Holt.

After the Civil War, Samuel Morrison, reporter for the *St. Louis Herald*, is sent west in search of more stories of conflict. When he reaches Bell's Landing one rainy night, he discovers that the *Roanoke*, captained by his friend Enoch Adams, is tied up there waiting out the storm. Most of the passengers are bound for a commemoration at the fort named for Major Charles Rawley, who, as a young Union officer during the war, had been taking 100 soldiers west by steamboat to fight the Indians. Every night a few of his men had deserted, and Rawley had felt he needed to do something drastic or no men would be left. He had picked out one man, accused him of intending to desert, held a trial, condemned him, and shot him. This had accomplished Rawley's purpose, but before they reached their destination, all but ten of the men were taken by General La Prade. Rawley and the ten had been aboard when the steamboat had to tie up, and Rawley had decided to march his men across country to Fort Standish. Readers are not sure exactly what happened after this point because several stories have been told, and Morrison hears yet another version when he secretly shares his cabin with a stowaway named Alex Selkirk, who claims to be the only survivor from Rawley's group and to have been mistaken for Rawley when he was found. At Fort Standish, he says, he was given command of the cavalry and joined General La Prade for an attack against the Sioux. He fell into disgrace when he ordered his men not to fire on Indian women and children and, as a result, a lot of warriors escaped. Morrison feels compelled to piece together the complex story: Who is Charles Rawley—hero worthy of having a fort named for him, or coward who disgraced himself and his army in battle with Indians at Killdeer Mountain? As the exercises at Fort Rawley are taking place, Selkirk appears and shouts that the speaker is not telling the truth; then he disappears. Mrs. Hardesty, a *Roanoke* passenger, is convinced that Selkirk is the husband whose remains she has come to find and take home for burial. She refuses to leave the area with Morrison, convinced her husband will return to her. Sometime later Morrison hears that he did.

This is an unusual story of mistaken identity set against a

realistic historical background. The author has a reputation for writing both excellent histories and novels about Indians and the West, and this is a very well-written and intriguing story with several well-developed characters.

Alex Selkirk's story of what happened to Rawley and the ten men on the way to Fort Standish is told on pages 66–78 and can be used as a booktalk.

In 1858 four adult Mormons and a baby girl were attacked by Indians in Salt Creek Canyon, in Arizona. The three men were killed, but the woman, although scalped, survived until she knew she had saved the child. The story is told in *Massacre at Salt Creek* by Blain M. Yorgason. In *The Way West* A. B. Guthrie has drawn a fine cast of characters and a superb picture of the harsh, faith-stretching journey by covered wagon from Independence, Missouri, across hot dusty prairie, shallow streams, dry sandy desert, roaring rivers, and rugged mountains to Oregon and the Willamette River Valley. Recommend it to senior high readers or the unusual junior high student.

Burch, Jennings

They Cage the Animals at Night. 1984.
New American Library.

Younger readers who loved the juvenile title *The Lottery Rose* by Irene Hunt will also like reading *They Cage the Animals at Night*. Both stories concern boys without adequate home care. When the author is eight-and-a-half his mother takes him to the Home of the Angels, an orphanage run by Roman Catholic nuns, leaving him without an explanation but saying she will be back. A very severe, unpleasant nun gives him a number and takes him to the dormitory, where a bed and a pair of pajamas are assigned to him. The next morning he is allowed no breakfast because he sits down at the table before given permission. Later, a boy named Mark tells Jennings that he has to learn the rules and then it will not be too bad. Mark has classes in the afternoon because he is a lifer, but Jennings, expected to return to his family, is considered a part-timer and has no classes. He gets behind in school and so has difficulty later. The second night a different nun has charge of the dormitory, and each child is given a stuffed animal to take to bed.

Jennings receives a fuzzy brown-and-white dog with floppy black ears, which he promptly names Doggie. The animals are collected as soon as the children are asleep, but later the nun lets Jennings keep Doggie. After a short stay the boy is sent to a foster home, where the woman is so unreasonably mean to him that after a few days her husband insists Jennings be returned to the institution. Soon after this Mrs. Burch comes for her son, and they return home. But the institutional experience is repeated again and again because Mrs. Burch is not well. Jennings's home situation is not much better than the foster homes in which he is placed. Several times he runs away from orphanages and takes refuge in the zoo, where he follows people about for the food they discard. When he is picked up by the police, he finds some of them are kind and others unsympathetic. Eventually the bus driver who drives him to school and becomes his friend adopts the family and helps them until Jennings and his younger brother finish high school. It has been a hard life, but he has kept Doggie with him wherever he has gone because Doggie is a comfort and a dependable friend.

This is a well-told, moving true story, and my young readers were enthusiastic about it.

Jennings's experiences at his first foster home can be used as a booktalk, pages 39–48. In another scene, Jennings, remembering what it is like to be a new boy in an orphanage, befriends the new arrival seated next to him at the table and suffers severely for his kindness, pages 90–101.

The sensitively written story A Shine of Rainbows by Lillam Beckwith tells of Thomas, a slight, bashful eight-year-old orphan boy taken in by a childless couple. Mairi, the mother, is a loving, happy person, but Sandy, her husband, is taciturn and undemonstrative. Thomas thrives so well under Mairi's tender care that when she dies, he can carry on until Sandy comes to accept him as his son. Find a Safe Place by Alex Lazzarino is a true story of four boys who are institutionalized only because there is no adult to care for them. A woman teacher becomes interested in one boy who is a good student and helps him and his buddy escape. They go to work on her brother's ranch and attend school. In time the other two boys join them. Three of these boys go on to successful careers. This is a favorite story

16

with young people. Also, see Charles Dickens's *Great Expectations*° for other stories of orphaned children.

Butler, Octavia E.

Kindred. 1979. Doubleday.

In this intriguing variation on the time-travel theme, Dana and Kevin Franklin, a biracial couple (Dana is black and Kevin, white) have finally sold enough stories after four years of struggling to become writers that they are able to buy a house. That is when a strange set of circumstances begins to happen. They are busy unpacking, sorting, and shelving books when Dana becomes dizzy and falls to her knees. The house, books, and Kevin vanish, and she finds herself on the ground under some trees beside a river. Near the middle of the stream a child is splashing and screaming. Dana runs into the water. When she reaches him, he is floating face down. She tows him to shore, where she applies artificial respiration until he begins to breathe, cough, and cry. Dana feels faint and hears a man's gruff voice demand, "What's going on here?" She looks around, and everything vanishes. She comes to in her own home. Kevin saw her disappear, and now here she is, wet and shaking with fear. Gradually she tells him what happened. Later things begin to blur around her again, and Kevin asks, "Is it happening again?" Dana vanishes. This time she comes to in the boy's room. He has set fire to the draperies with a smoldering stick from the fireplace and is watching them burn. Dana catches the unburned part and throws the whole drapery out the window. The boy is three or four years older than when she last saw him; she asks the date, and he tells her it is 1815. She expects to vanish again and return to Kevin, but it doesn't happen. The boy, Rufus, tells her where to find a freeborn black girl and her mother, who could help her. When Dana draws near the cabin, she sees some white men drag a black man from the cabin, tie him to a tree, and whip him. Then they ride off, half dragging the slave behind them. Later one of the men returns. While Dana is fighting him off, she loses consciousness and comes to at home with Kevin. Altogether she makes six trips back in time. It seems that whenever Rufus needs help, she goes to him. After he dies, she no longer goes back.

The story is convincing, and the characters are interesting.

The picture of the life for slaves on a small plantation is realistic. The girls in my group liked the story very much, and the librarians recommended it highly.

Dana's first visit to the world of pre–Civil War days should be enough to interest young people in reading the book, pages 12–17.

In *The Last Day of Creation* by Wolfgang Jeschke, the U.S. Navy is sending men back in time 5½ million years to the Mediterranean, which in those days was a desert. The men were to explore for the oil that today is controlled by the Arabs and to build a pipeline into present-day Europe. But things do not work out as they expect. Also suggest Clifford D. Simak's *Special Deliverance*, in which Edward Lansing, a college professor in a sleepy New England town, time travels with four persons and a robot from other worlds to a world that is in ruins and whose population has disappeared. They want to know why they are there and when they can return home, but they meet no one who can answer questions. Four of the six do not survive their ordeals. *The Time Machine* by H. G. Wells, another tale of travel through time, tells of the Time Traveler going ahead in time to the year 802,701. In the area around the Thames he finds two types of people—beautiful, fragile, but shallow beings who are abroad only in daylight, and subterranian night creatures who have an apelike appearance. In *Time after Time*, Allen Appel takes his main character, Alex Balfour, from the present to Russia during World War I several times. There Alex becomes involved in the murder of Rasputin, exposes Mata Hari, has knowledge of the Zimmerman epistle, and tries to rescue members of the royal family from execution. Like Dana and Kevin in *Kindred*, Alex is living with a girl. In Russia he has a sexual encounter with a woman colleague.

Card, Orson Scott

Ender's Game.   1977.   Tom Doherty Associates.

In Card's award-winning science fiction novel, Ender Wiggin has been carefully monitored for three years. When he is six years old, Colonel Graff, director of primary training at Battle School in the Belt, informs the boy's parents that Ender has been accepted as a student. Because Ender injures a

18

boy who torments him on the voyage to the Belt, he enters the new school with some enemies, but he soon shows himself to be more clever and ingenious than his classmates, and most change their opinion of him. Divided into teams, the students fight one another in a gravity-free battleroom with weapons that paralyze temporarily. Almost immediately Ender figures out techniques that enable his team to win, and in time his group far outshines the others. The teachers, not satisfied, come up with new ideas and requirements for battles, but Ender outthinks them all, developing excellent platoon leaders and holding many practice sessions. The teachers try to wear out Ender and his team by having them fight every day, then twice a day, and finally against two opposing teams at the same time. Ender's team always wins. When he is ten, he is promoted to Command School on Eros, but, tired out from fighting against such odds, Ender is dispirited and lonely. Also, Command School is grueling. There he has no personal contact with students his age and fighting is done by simulator. It helps, however, when Ender discovers that his team has followed him to Eros. His instructor drives him so hard that he begins to make mistakes in judgment; he still wins but suffers bigger losses. He knows they are being prepared to fight an enemy—known as the buggers—that has superior equipment and numbers. On the day of his final exam, the enemy, which appears on the simulator, outnumbers him a thousand to one. There is only one chance for victory, he takes it, and the enemy disintegrates. It is then that Ender learns that his battle was not make-believe but the real thing.

Readers become so sympathetic toward Ender, separated from his family and friends at age six, that they feel compelled to find out what happened to him. My young readers highly recommend the book. The suspense is well maintained. Except where appropriate to the circumstance, the narrative is free from coarseness and vulgar dialogue.

Try the following scenes for booktalking: Ender does not have an easy life in his school on earth or at home, pages 6–15. Ender's experience on the shuttle to Battle School is found on pages 31–35. These examples win the reader's sympathy and interest.

Another story in which the brightest and most talented children have a chance to develop under expert guidance is *Earth-*

child by Sharon Webb. Children can choose immortality and have an important role in space, or they can choose mortality and develop a special talent, as in music, dance, or art, on earth. The sequels are not as good as the first book. Another story about an unusually intelligent and capable child is found in *Emergence* by David Palmer. Candy, an eleven-year-old *Homo post hominem,* is totally immune to human disease and vastly superior in every way to *Homo sapiens* children. She survives worldwide biological warfare in a shelter deep under her parents' home, and in time she searches for and finds survivors of her own species and undertakes to defuse the bomb programmed in outer space to attack the area where the *Homo post hominems* have congregated in the United States. This is a very long and detailed but fascinating story. In *Still River* Hal Clement describes the activities of five inhabitants from different planets who are students working for a prestigious degree. They are deposited by a school ship on Enigma 88, a tiny, uninhabited planet. Unexpected discoveries endanger the group, and only by close cooperation do they survive.

Chao, Evelina

Gates of Grace. 1985. Warner.

When Mei-yu married Kung-chiao, her father disowned her for marrying beneath her social class. An excellent student, Kung-chiao wanted to continue his education in the United States away from Communist domination, and the young couple settled in New York City's Chinatown. Kung-chiao finds part-time work, and Mei-yu's skill with a needle is soon discovered by Madame Peng, owner of a clothing shop for women. The young couple have a baby girl whom they name Fernadina. But shortly before Kung-chiao is to graduate, he is murdered on the street. Everyone suspects a man thought to have connections with the underworld. Since housing is scarce in Chinatown, Mei-yu is forced to move, and Madame Peng lets her have a one-room apartment she keeps for visitors. With Mei-yu's designing and needlework in increasing demand, Madame Peng decides to open a shop in Washington, D.C., where her son, Richard, practices law. She sends Mei-yu there as head seamstress. Though her son has fallen in love and intends to marry Lilliam Chin, an attaché at the Chinese Embassy, Madame Peng does not approve. Soon Miss Chin returns to Taiwan. After a few months Richard begins to invite Mei-yu and Fernadina to go sightseeing. Although the little girl does not like him, Mei-yu and Richard are eventually married, and he establishes his own law office. Madame Peng is happy with the marriage and overjoyed when they have a son. Fernadina is growing up; she is a very good student, but she feels lonely and unappreciated. Her relationship with her mother had been so close before the marriage. At the end, when Fernadina enrolls at Barnard in New York City, she learns something about her father's death that gives the story a surprise ending.

The novel is a bit involved, but it is so well done and the characters are so interesting that it is difficult to put the book down. The close relationships among the members of an old Chinese family and their sense of integrity, responsibility, and devotion to parents is heartwarming—though perhaps surprising to modern-day young people. Also, the story brings out the prejudice that the various Chinese characters encounter from white Americans.

For a booktalk use the surprise dinner party Mei-yu plans for her husband on the night he finishes his last exam. This is a good chance to introduce the young couple's friends, pages 55, 62–65, 67–71.

Young people who have enjoyed reading Laurence Yep's *Dragonwings*, the story of a Chinese boy and his father in San Francisco in the early 1900s, might like to read this story of a little Chinese girl and her mother.

Ching, Lucy

One of the Lucky Ones. 1982. Doubleday.

Lucy Ching is blinded at six months of age when her mother takes her to a herbalist for treatment of her eyes. Blind people in China had always been outcasts in society, and blind girls were often sold as slaves to become beggars, singers, or prostitutes, working for their owners. However, because Lucy's family is quite well off, they can keep her at home with an amah to care for her. One day when she is eight, she hears on the radio that blind children in America can learn to read, and she asks her older brother, a ham radio operator, to get information for her. A doctor in Manila hears the boy's question on the air, and two months later a package arrives containing a braille handframe and a stylus as well as cards giving the letters of the English alphabet and some words in braille. Lucy knows the English alphabet from hearing her brother and sister do their homework, and she begins to teach herself to write in braille. This is just the beginning. Next comes the Cantonese braille alphabet and an interest in the Christian religion. In church one day, a Chinese middle school teacher speaks to Lucy, and the child tells her that she can read and write in English and Cantonese braille and wants to go to school with other children. The woman promises to investigate. The teachers decide to let Lucy try attending classes for three months; her father will have to pay her school fees. Her amah, Ah Wor, who has encouraged her from the beginning, tells her that she can have her life savings if need be. Lucy takes an entrance exam and is admitted. There are problems: finding people to read the textbooks to her, taking an examination, finding out what the teacher has written on the blackboard, and studying the notes she has taken in class. But Lucy does well and stays on at school. In her third year the Communists take over Canton, and the family has to leave, taking only their clothing with them. Most of the servants are dismissed because her father has no job and little money. The family ends up in Macao, where Lucy's father finds part-time work, and Ah Wor is able to get outwork from a factory and contribute to the family income. Again Lucy looks for a school. Because of her courage and ingenuity, she finds not only a school but also the money for expenses. To graduate she finally has to attend school in Hong Kong, and she and Ah Wor manage even that. Then she is offered a scholarship to study at the Perkins Institution for the Blind in Massachusetts, where she will be trained to teach other blind people. Ah Wor is still with her.

It seems almost incredible that a blind child in China could accomplish what Lucy did because, except for Ah Wor, no one encouraged her or was interested in her progress. This autobiography is detailed, and the reader learns a great deal about Chinese customs, manners, family life, and education, and a little of the country's history. The selflessness of Ah Wor is unusual, and she is particularly well drawn.

In a booktalk use pages 1–4, in which Lucy receives her introduction to braille. Indicate that there was no stopping this child from then on, even though her parents did not approve of what she was doing.

Although Hsiau-yen does not have to cope with the Chinese attitude toward blindness, she has other problems that call for independent thinking and action if she is to make an unencumbered life for herself. She tells her story in *Second Daughter* by Katherine (her American name) Wei. *Vedi* is quite a different story of a blind child in an Asian country. In it Ved Mehta tells of being sent at the age of five to a school for the blind in Bombay, India, 1,300 miles from his family. His father wants him to be educated and independent. Except for vacations he spends four years there growing quite self-reliant, thus preparing himself to go alone to the United States for further education.

Christie, Agatha

And Then There Were None. 1940. Dodd, Mead.

Eight persons, unknown to one another, are invited for a visit to Indian Island off the coast of Devon. Each invitation is worded in such a way that its recipient will most likely accept. When those invited reach their destination, they find that the host and hostess have not yet returned to the island but that the guests' needs will be amply supplied by a well-trained butler and a good cook, Mr. and Mrs. Rogers. The guests find in their rooms a copy of the nursery rhyme "Ten Little Indians," and ten little china Indians are in the center of the dining room table. After an excellent dinner, the guests gather in the drawing room for coffee. Suddenly a loud voice addresses them, naming each guest and the two servants, together with the names of the persons each has allegedly murdered. Upset and indignant, the visitors protest their innocence. Finding that the voice came from a record player in the next room, the guests begin to discuss the situation, their invitations, and the accusations. Anthony Marston admits to killing two young people with his car, but he has not been held responsible for the deaths. Another guest admits to abandoning twenty-one members of an East African tribe when his party became lost and was short of food. A few minutes later Marston is dead, apparently having choked on his drink, but Dr. Armstrong, another guest, says Marston has been poisoned. One by one over the next few days the other guests are picked off, and the death of each matches the removal of one of the little Indians in the nursery rhyme. Also, each time, a china Indian disappears from the table. With each death those remaining become more wary of one another and more terrified. Finally, the last one dies. The boatman, who had brought the guests to the island, discovers the bodies and summons the police who are unable to determine the murderer's identity. The mystery would remain unsolved had not the murderer put his confession in a bottle and thrown it into the sea, where it eventually was found. He had felt great satisfaction in planing the perfect crime.

This is a well-plotted mystery with suspicion cast on first one and then another, so that the identity of the guilty one is a surprise at the end. The suspense is high and well maintained. All were guilty of the murder of which they were accused; their guilt hangs just below the surface of their minds, worrying and tormenting them.

A booktalk can include the nursery rhyme, page 48 (paperback), and the loud-voiced accusations from the record player, page 35 (paperback). This is perhaps more than enough to rouse interest.

Suggest as follow-ups other murder mysteries by Christie. *Murder on the Orient Express* concerns twelve persons who wish to see a man dead and tells how they go about making their wish come true. In *Evil under the Sun* a small number of guests are assembled at an inn on a tiny island off the English coast; among them are Hercule Poirot, the famous Belgian detective, and Arlena Stuart, a former actress who is found strangled. In *The A.B.C. Murders* Hercule Poirot receives a letter signed A.B.C., telling him that a crime will be committed on June 21 in Andover and suggesting Poirot cannot solve it. Miss Jane Marple is the wise old lady whom Christie used to solve some of her mysteries, among them, *The Body in the Library.* When a dead girl is found in Colonel Bantry's library early one morning, his wife immediately calls her friend Jane. Obviously the colonel is not the murderer, but it takes a while for Miss Marple to untangle the web of mystery and reveal the guilty persons.

Clarke, Arthur C.

2010: Odyssey Two.   1982.   Ballantine.

This sequel to *2001: A Space Odyssey* tells the story of the Russian ship *Leonov,* which reaches the vicinity of Jupiter, where the abandoned U.S. ship *Discovery* is in orbit. Drs. Heywood Floyd, Chandra, and Walter Curnow, each of whom have had important roles on the *Discovery,* have been invited to join the *Leonov.* The three men have been given injections so that they can hibernate until the *Leonov* reaches its destination in ten months' time. However, Heywood is awakened a month early when it is discovered that a Chinese ship is enroute to Jupiter and will probably reach the planet before the Russians do. The Chinese do not go into orbit around Jupiter after all, but shoot past, and Heywood guesses they will land on Europa, where they can take on enough water to allow them to cruise wherever they like. Heywood is correct, but the Chinese are never to leave Europa. A Chinese message being sent in code is interrupted suddenly, and a bit later the *Leonov* picks up a message for Dr. Floyd from the lone survivor saying the Chinese ship has been destroyed by a strange life form. The *Leonov* successfully goes into orbit around Io, from which they make contact with *Discovery.* Walter Curnow's job is to board the revolving ship and bring it under control, with help from the Russian structural engineer. They find the power system intact and the fuel sufficient for the return journey to earth. Dr. Chandra's duty is to reactivate Hal, the computer, which he does. Both ships can then return to an orbit around Jupiter, where there is a slab nicknamed Big Brother that resembles exactly, except for its huge size, a small slab found on the moon. The moon slab, named TMA-1, had at one time directed a signal to Jupiter. David Bowman had been the last survivor on the *Discovery,* and no one knows what happened to him. The author at this point gives some idea of Bowman's experiences. Although he died, his spirit lives on to make some strange voyages, and it contacts Dr. Floyd to tell him that the *Leonov* must leave the vicinity of Jupiter within fifteen days. Floyd has trouble convincing the captain that he has spoken with Bowman, but eventually events point to the wisdom of an early departure. Shortly after they leave, a vast explosion changes the arrangement of that part of the heavens.

Librarians across the United States who were consulted said that this book is very popular with their readers. The idea of cooperation between the Russians and Americans is something to contemplate. Clarke has produced some interesting characters, and their experiences seem logical and are quite fascinating.

In a booktalk, set the scene on the *Leonov*, then use chapter 11, in which Professor Chang from the Chinese spaceship reports the events that destroyed their vessel and crew. Clarke's *2061: Odyssey Three* is a natural follow-up. In it, Heywood Floyd takes part in an expedition to Halley's Comet, a mission cut short when a sister ship crashes on Europa, the one world forbidden to humans by the alien Monoliths.

Douglas Adams, in *A Hitchhiker's Guide to the Galaxy*, has let his imagination run away and has compiled the experiences of two young men—one an inhabitant of another planet—who escape from Earth just as it is destroyed and stow away on a spaceship. They are discovered, cast out into space, and rescued by another ship. They visit another planet and have some outlandish adventures. Teens find this very entertaining. The eight stories and one movie outline that compose Clarke's *The Sentinel* represent his published writing of science fiction from 1945 to 1979. The stories tell of the exploration of and adventures on distant moons and planets as well as on earth. This may serve to introduce readers to other books of short science fiction stories. Ron Miller and Williams Hartmann, authors of *The Grand Tour: A Traveler's Guide to the Solar System*, introduce the reader to the planets and smaller worlds beginning with the largest, Jupiter. They describe each and tell what has been discovered about them by telescope and by photographs taken by *Voyager 1* and *2*, *Viking 1* and *2*, and *Apollo 11, 12*, and *15*. It is a very attractive and intriguing introduction to a fascinating subject. Carl Sagan's *Cosmos* is truly an engrossing book for anyone interested in the evolution of the earth, its history, and the people who contributed to our growing knowledge of it. It also provides information on the planets, galaxies, and stars. The book is enhanced by full-color illustrations and photographs.

Clarkson, Ewan

The Wake of the Storm. 1983. St. Martin's.

When Scarr's wife died leaving him childless at the age of forty, he sold his veterinary practice and his house and moved to a small farm, where he had lived for four years when the story opens. To supplement his small income, he raises vegetables, hens, ducks, and geese, which he sells in the nearby village. The author alternates Scarr's story with those of two otters and a salmon on its way to spawn. A storm is brewing, and when it strikes, it is a bad one. A girl on a motorbike is hugging the white line on the narrow, deserted road when suddenly a humped, black shape darts in front of her. She jams on her brakes and swerves toward the edge of the road. The next thing she knows she is in a ditch with water over her head. She manages to retrieve her duffle bag and crawl up to the shoulder of the road. There lies the male otter she struck, its back legs useless. When she reaches out her hand, it bites her. Dumping her belongings out of her bag, she grabs the otter's tail and stuffs him into the bag, but not before being bitten twice. Her bike is disabled, but luckily she is near Scarr's house, and she knocks on his door before collapsing against it. After he cleans her up and takes care of her bites, she tells him her name is Dawn and that an injured otter is in her bag. He calls the doctor for the girl and the veterinarian for the animal. The latter is a young man, Brian Beck, with whom Scarr has become friends. As soon as Dawn is stronger, she goes out to the barn to see the otter and asks Scarr if she can stay a while and help with the work around the house and garden. The otter is recovering from its injury; Scarr thinks it should be returned to the wild, and Dawn agrees. Through the license number of the bike, Brian finds out who Dawn is, and he and Scarr remember reading about her family in the newspaper. Brian has been making friendly calls on Dawn, and finally Scarr tells her that they know who she is and that there was no reason for her to assume her father's difficulty as her burden. At the end, she and Brian are married, and Scarr is alone again.

Clarkson is a conservationist and a photographer of wildlife, and in his earlier years was a veterinarian. Thus, it is not surprising that readers learn a little about the earth and its inhabitants, animals and humans, as they read about some very appealing characters.

In a booktalk, introduce Dawn and tell what happened to her in the storm, pages 39–57.

The following could also be suggested: *Thistle and Co.* by Era Zistel tells of several wild animals that became her friends. Thistle, a baby raccoon found in a wet roadside ditch and nursed back to health, returned to the wild when it matured but remained friends with the author. A rescued baby skunk grew up to be a household pet for some time before it disappeared. A nature photographer and a broadcaster, a meteorologist and a pilot, Dan True saw a mother eagle shot down by a passenger in a Piper Cub. Dan rescued her two eggs, but only one hatched. In *Flying Free* he tells of raising that eagle and trying to teach it to hunt for itself and live in the wild. In *A Family of Eagles,* True watches a pair of eagles court. When the male, which he had raised, has built their nest, Dan establishes his blind so that he can observe the female setting, the hatching, and the development of the chicks. In *Some of My Best Friends Are Animals,* Terry Murphy, the director of the Dublin Zoo, tells of many experiences—humorous, exciting, dangerous, and just plain interesting—with animal residents of his domain.

Cousteau, Jacques-Yves, with *Frederic Dumas*

The Silent World.   1953.   Harper.

Although Cousteau's newer books are fascinating to read, they do not strike immediate fire as does this older title. The beginning paragraph, when the author and his friends unpack the first aqualung, captures the readers' attention, and interest never wanes. Here is all the excitement of science fiction along with the reality of the here and now. Here is a high-spirited, adventure-packed, personal narrative of undersea salvage, scientific research, and exploration in the Mediterranean. With aqualungs (of which Cousteau was co-inventor), he and his men dived nearly naked into pressures that have crushed submarines. Cousteau describes what it is like to be a "manfish" swimming with sharks, mantas, and octopuses. The dives made by the Undersea Research Group to locate and explore wrecks (some had sunk during World War II and one went down about 80 B.C.) taught them a lot about work at great depths. The group also hunted unexploded mines after World War II. One of the most exciting chapters is "Cave Diving," in which Cousteau tells how they nearly lost their lives penetrating the Fountain of Vaucluse. Another provides an account of Cousteau's audacious fifty-fathom dive into the zone of rapture, where divers become like drunken gods because of the pressure, and of the 396-foot dive that took a brave companion's life. What began as curiosity about the unknown beneath the sea developed into serious oceanographic study, of which his later books are a result.

Young people who like sea stories or who have had some experiences with snorkels and fins are intrigued with the descriptions of underwater forms of life. Underwater exploration calls for close camaraderie among divers, constant vigilance, physical fitness, and high courage.

In addition to the incidents mentioned above, there are many others worth recounting: Dumas's dive on a sunken wreck, pages 44–46, and the encounter with man-eating sharks, pages 223–33, are two.

Cousteau has written individual books on whales, dolphins, octopuses, and other creatures of the deep, all of which are recommended. *The Living Sea*, which Cousteau wrote ten years after *The Silent World*, gives additional information on underseas exploration. Frederic Dumas, a professional diver who often works and writes with Cousteau, has collected his diving experiences in *30 Centuries under the Sea*. In an enthralling story, *Man: 1200 Years under the Sea*, Robert E. Burgess begins with the discovery of a Roman ship loaded with wine and Greek statues sunk about 86 B.C. and continues with ships sunk in many other seas. He tells how new technological aids have helped in the recovery of ships and cargos. *A Matter of Risk* by Roy Varner and Wayne Collier reveals the story of the *Hughes Glomar Explorer*, the huge ship built to salvage a Russian submarine that sank three miles deep in the ocean north of Hawaii. The CIA wished to get valuable information. The account tells of the ship's construction, the training of the crews, and the salvage operation. This book is for the exceptional reader.

Cragg, Sheila

Run, Patty, Run. 1980. Harper and Row.

This is an incredible but true story of a girl who refuses to let a handicap defeat her and of the family who supports her in every way they can. The doctor has always diagnosed Patty's seizures over the first years of her life as convulsions resulting from a fever. However, when the child is in sixth grade, the doctor tells Dotty, her mother, that Patty has epilepsy. At the time epilepsy seems something of which to be ashamed. The neighborhood youngsters do not want her to take part in their games because she is inept, and sometimes girls with whom she has been friends prefer to exclude her. Patty is hurt. Her father, Jim, encourages her to run because he can run with her, and they are the best of friends. She tries to run a mile a day. Then in 1974 she and Jim decide to run to grandmother's house on New Year's Day, a distance of thirty miles, and Patty is able to do it. In March, 1975, Patty and Jim enter the Los Angeles Marathon, and although they come in last, they feel satisfaction. When she is thirteen, she enters a 100-mile run to San Diego. This is quite an adventure and another milestone on Patty's road to success. Dotty is in the van and meets them at predetermined locations with food and accommodations for rest and sleep. Jim writes to *Runner's World* inquiring about the long-distance running record for a woman and learns it is 100 miles. Patty could have broken that at San Diego if she had run two more miles. The fall that Patty enters high school, she and Jim decide to run to Las Vegas during Christmas vacation. They do it but decide to spend Christmas at home in the future. During her sophomore year Patty's experiences persuade her to admit to the world that she has epilepsy. Her family acquiesce, and Jim calls the Orange County Epilepsy Society. They are excited about having Patty make her next long run for them. That is to San Francisco, 502.18 miles, and it draws national attention. In 1978 Patty runs from Minneapolis to Washington, D.C. in ninety-two days, covering 2,009.4 miles.

The description of Jim and Patty's first run to grandmother's house is short and could be used as a booktalk after introducing Patty and her disability, pages 29–31. Girls especially seem to like stories of handicapped persons who have conquered or learned to live with their disabilities. If junior high school readers like the following juvenile titles, the librarian can suggest the adult titles. *Marathon Miranda* by Elizabeth Winthrop tells of a girl who had asthma and trained to run in a marathon, thus making headway in overcoming her handicap. In *A Handful of Stars* Barbara Girion has written of a high school sophomore who begins to have epileptic seizures and has to learn to live with her handicap.

Another handicapped girl's story is told in *Geri* by Geri Jewell. She decided early that she wanted a career on the stage, but no one believed a girl with cerebral palsy could achieve that. She had to grow up emotionally, and when she painfully began to make progress, opportunities came to her. In *They Accepted the Challenge* Charles Kuntzleman tells the true stories of eighteen persons from the teens to the eighties who overcame their handicaps. Several became runners, but others accomplished their goals by swimming, exercising, walking, and eating the right food. All had excellent mental attitudes. In *The Mike King Story* Mike tells about his trip in his wheelchair on the highway between Fairbanks, Alaska, and Washington, D.C., in 1985. On the way he raised money for organizations for the handicapped and rehabilitation centers.

Crane, Stephen

The Red Badge of Courage.   1895.

Fascinated by the glamour and excitement of uniforms and combat, Henry Fleming, a young farm boy, eagerly enlists as a Union private during the Civil War. He finds himself in a raw, new regiment, eventually bored by inaction but frightened by the conversations about fighting. The men boast at first about the heroic deeds they will do, but as time drags on and they see no action, they become less and less certain of their glorious conduct under battle stress. Restlessness, loneliness, and apprehension pass in waves over Henry. How will he react to the command to charge? When the first call to march comes, everyone is hilarious, but gradually their enthusiasm dulls as their feet begin to hurt and they grow tired and hungry. Suddenly the hours of waiting are over, and they are fighting. The battle is fierce at first; panic strikes the men as the enemy pushes them back. Gradually one man after another takes to his heels, and Henry, too, turns to run away. He loses his gun, but he keeps going and soon loses touch with his regiment. Overcome by remorse and the shame of cowardice, he envies the wounds of combatants whom he joins behind the battle zone. Ironically he achieves his "red badge of courage" when another retreating soldier hits him over the head with his rifle in a moment of panic. After finding his direction and renewing his courage, Henry rejoins his outfit. All around there are pockets of firing; then the battle breaks out again in earnest. Dog-tired and battle weary, the men are inclined to hide behind trees and let the enemy hunt them. Suddenly a hatred of the victorious enemy wells up in Henry, and from then on he fights like a wildcat, gaining the epithet "war devil." Remorse fades as he retrieves the regimental flag from the dying color sergeant and helps rally the men. With a new sense of assurance he faces the future as a man who has "been to touch the great death and found that, after all, it was but the great death."

A living, readable story of the effect of war on a sensitive mind, this classic has literary excellence plus sound psychological insights. Both boys and girls are deeply moved by the book. It has the perpetual reality of youth with its resilience and resourcefulness. The mother's parting advice in chapter 1 could have been given in any century, and the boy's progression to self-understanding is unbelievably realistic.

The occasion of Henry's going to war, chapter 1, and the flight before enemy guns, chapters 6 and 7, can be worked into a booktalk.

Also suggest *April Morning* by Howard Fast, which tells of a boy's first taste of battle at the beginning of the American Revolution. *Hacey Miller* by James Sherburne tells of another boy who begins to take a stand against slavery when he is only thirteen and whose conviction grows through pre–Civil War days when he is in college. *The Way to Fort Pillow* continues Hacey's story during the war when he fights for the Union against family, friends, and relatives. Refer to Douglas Jones on page 84 for other books about young men in the Civil War.

D'Ambrosio, Richard

No Language but a Cry.   1970.   Doubleday.

The author, a psychoanalyst, tells the story of a girl named Laura who is born to alcoholic and paranoid schizophrenic parents. As a baby Laura cries often, and when she is one-and-a-half years old, her exasperated parents place her in a large frying pan on a hot stove. The child's screams prompt a neighbor to call the police, who take the tot to the hospital. Later her parents are placed in a mental institution. When Dr. D'Ambrosio comes to know her, Laura has been in a hospital and children's shelter for five years and in a Catholic home for girls from broken homes for seven years. She is scarred, crippled, mute, friendless, and mostly unresponsive to the nuns who care for her. The doctor describes in considerable detail the methods he uses to rouse the child's interest as she sits hunched in her chair, never looking at him or apparently hearing him as he talks to her. He meets Laura twice a week, sometimes taking her for a walk. After many weeks she demonstrates that she trusts him a little when some boys on roller skates threaten to attack her. Then she clings to the doctor. During his second year with her he slowly assembles a dollhouse of interlocking plastic bricks and is encouraged by some show of interest on Laura's part. As he is arranging the furniture, she actually takes part in that activity, but there is no further show of interest that year. During the third year he begins to act out episodes with a family of dolls in the dollhouse. This leads to his making a mock-up of the building in which Laura had lived with her parents, and he begins to play-act with two doll parents and a doll baby, doing as Laura and her parents probably had done. D'Ambrosio is determined to shock the girl out of her lethargy, and he does. When the doll parents begin to beat the baby, Laura begins to shout "No! No!" She grabs the dolls and pounds them to pieces. Then she collapses, sobbing in his arms. From that point on there is progress, although there are setbacks and rebellion at times. At the end, Laura graduates from high school, takes training for a career as a baby nurse, and launches out on her own.

This well-written, moving account is quite shocking and dramatic at times. That Dr. D'Ambrosio was a patient and persistent man is evidenced by the years he spent straightening out this child. The love, concern, and efficiency of the nuns are heartening to those who know something of the needs of children from broken homes.

A short booktalk can include part of the foregoing annotation.

In *A Circle of Children* by Mary McCracken, a teacher states how she worked with four children at a time in a special school to help rid them of their fears so that they could cope with new learning experiences. She describes in *Lovey, a Very Special Child* how she helped a very difficult little girl and kept working with the three boys who appeared in the earlier title. In *A Different Drum* Constance Cameron, a mother, tells how she carefully, lovingly, and patiently taught her aphasic son the words and concepts that normal children learn by themselves. She explains in detail the techniques she used until the boy could assume his place in a classroom with his peers. Also see Tory Hayden's *One Child°* for similar books.

Dickens, Charles

Great Expectations. [1895].

Philip Pirrip, known as Pip, is orphaned as a small child and grudgingly "brought up by hand" by his older sister and her husband. They live in a small English village in the marsh country, only twenty miles from the sea, where a prison ship is anchored. One Christmas Eve when Pip is visiting the cemetery, he is accosted by a rough-looking stranger who demands that the boy bring him food and a file to cut the iron chain that binds his leg. Pip obliges, and the escaped convict promises Pip that someday he will reward him for his help. Sometime later Pip is sent on an errand to Satis House, the gloomy mansion of the eccentric Miss Havisham. Here he finds an old, white-haired lady living in a darkened house where all the clocks were stopped on the day her bridegroom failed to appear for the wedding ceremony. The only ray of sunshine in the dismal place is the lovely but haughty Estelle, whom Miss Havisham has adopted, hoping that eventually the little girl will break the hearts of many men as a kind of repayment for the old lady's own suffering. Pip is invited to come to the house regularly, and Estelle begins early to make the opposite sex unhappy, for she enjoys teasing her shy playmate. At fourteen Pip is apprenticed to his brother-in-law Joe and spends four years learning the trade of blacksmith. One day Mr. Jaggers, a lawyer from London whom Pip has seen at Miss Havisham's, comes to tell the boy that he is to inherit a handsome sum of money and must prepare himself by becoming a gentleman. He is to go to London, where arrangements have been made for a relative of Miss Havisham to tutor him. Although the benefactor's name is not revealed, Pip thinks that it must be the old lady herself; later he discovers that it is the old convict, Magwitch, whom he had befriended. Magwitch, after regaining his freedom, worked very hard to get the money to make Pip a gentleman, risking great dangers to return to England and enjoy the realization of his dream. Although Pip feels only abhorrence and repugnance toward the old man and is determined to get him out of the country and end their relationship, he does recognize the great debt he owes the old convict and makes elaborate plans to smuggle him out to France. When the plan fails, his benefactor is taken to prison, tried, and condemned to die; his fortune is forfeited to the Crown, leaving Pip penniless again.

Good readers who like long, adventurous, romantic novels enjoy this classic.

A good booktalk can consist of the introduction of the main characters and information from chapters 7 and 9 describing Miss Havisham's unhappy situation.

This story can be a good introduction to Dickens and can be followed by *Oliver Twist* and *David Copperfield*. Trained to be a pickpocket, the boy Oliver has a hard time breaking away from the criminal environment. David, a poor boy and out of work at an early age, runs away to his great aunt's home where he has a chance for some education and a better type of work. Set at the time of the French Revolution, *A Tale of Two Cities* is more than a story of a poor boy's success. It concerns the daughter of a man unjustly imprisoned in the Bastille for twenty years and the young man who loves and marries her. His aristocratic family's arrogance and misdeeds bring the death sentence on him. It is also a story of the self-sacrifice of a friend, who takes his place at the guillotine at the last moment.

Doyle, Arthur Conan

The Complete Sherlock Holmes.   1930.   Doubleday.

This volume contains not only Sherlock Holmes's *Adventures* and *Memoirs* but also *A Study in Scarlet, The Sign of the Four, Hound of the Baskervilles, The Valley of Fear, His Last Bow,* and *The Case Book.* Holmes was seldom unsuccessful in a case, but in "A Scandal in Bohemia" he is bested by a woman's wit while trying to recover a photograph that could injure a client if publicized. In contrast, in "A Case of Identity" the famous detective is so quick that he really solves the mystery of the disappearance of his client's fiance before the young woman has left his room on Baker Street. In "The Bascombe Valley Mystery" circumstantial evidence seems to indicate that Tom McCarthy killed his own father, but Holmes comes up with enough objections to the evidence to get Tom off. Holmes had a good reason for not disclosing the name of the murderer. In "The Adventure of the Illustrious Client" Holmes is asked to find a way to prevent the marriage of Miss Violet de Merville to Baron Gruner, who is known to be guilty of many crimes but is thought by his fiancee to be maligned. Mr. Holmes succeeds. The murderers that Holmes exposes are not always humans. In "Silver Blaze" he discovers that the killer of trainer John Straker is the horse he had been about to mutilate. In the somewhat amusing "Man with the Twisted Lip" a woman comes to the detective asking him to find her husband, a well-to-do businessman. She says she had glimpsed him in a strange place in deshabille and he had not been seen since. Holmes quickly locates him, and the man confesses that, although his wife thinks he is in business, he makes more money as a disfigured beggar on the street than he would in business. In "The Adventure of the Dancing Men" a country gentleman comes to Holmes with a piece of paper on which are stick figures in various poses. No sense can be made of the figures, but the man's wife evidently knows what they mean because she appears frightened. Eventually Holmes solves the case, but he's a little too late to prevent the client's death.

Those who like mysteries solved by deduction are fond of Sherlock Holmes. They also pick up, perhaps unconsciously, a wealth of other information. The detective is especially popular with boys.

For a booktalk, tell one of the stories completely. Young people resent learning just the facts first told to Holmes by the client and nothing about his solving the case.

As a follow-up suggest *Murder Most Irregular* by H. Paul Jeffers. Before the Baker Street Irregulars' annual dinner in honor of Sherlock Holmes is held at the Queen Victoria Hotel in New York City, seven of the men receive threatening letters. One man is shot in the back on his way to the dinner, and another beats off two men who attack him with sticks. Detective David Morgan is hired to find the murderer, but he does not until after two more men die. Also see *And Then There Were None*° by Agatha Christie and *The Danger*° by Dick Francis. In *Sherlock Holmes and the Case of the Raleigh Legacy*, L. B. Greenwood, following Arthur Conan Doyle's style of writing, presents the famous detective and Dr. Watson working to solve a mystery involving a college friend of Watson's who is heir to a legacy outlined in a letter written in the 1600s. It takes many weeks to interpret the letter's obscure references.

DuMaurier, Daphne

Rebecca.   1938.   Doubleday.

The heroine of this book is such a gauche, shy, quiet person that even though she is a young woman and the hired companion of a well-to-do, social-climbing American, Mrs. Van Hopper, she is considered a child, and the author does not give the reader her name. At first it is difficult to understand why wealthy young man-of-the-world Maxim de Winter would ask such an immature, inexperienced young woman to marry him, but he does, and she accepts. Disappointed at losing her aide, Mrs. Van Hopper is blunt and says he is marrying her because he cannot go on living alone at Manderley, his lovely family home in England, after losing his first wife so tragically. At Manderley the new Mrs. de Winter feels she is compared constantly to the beautiful, vivacious, accomplished Rebecca, Maxim's first wife, and this makes her more self-conscious and more prone to stiffness and to social errors. Mrs. Danvers, the housekeeper who had been devoted to Rebecca, seems to do everything she can to belittle her new mistress and make her feel unwanted and uncomfortable. The hostility culminates in her suggestion for Mrs. de Winter's costume for the

Manderley fancy-dress ball. Delighted with herself for once, and eager to please her husband, the new bride does not know that the reaction to her appearance will be violent. Rebecca had worn an identical dress to her last ball, the night before her death. The next day when a ship runs aground in a heavy fog on the reef at the entrance to Manderley's bay, a diver, sent down to discover the extent of the damage, discovers Rebecca's sunken boat, and the body in the cabin is identified as hers. It is then that Maxim confesses to his wife what his marriage to Rebecca had really been like and the part he had played in her death. From that point on, the story reads like a murder mystery, and new light is thrown on the opening chapter, which seems a bit vague on first reading.

It is easy for girls to see themselves as the young heroine of this story, and it is fascinating for them to ponder what they would have done in her shoes. The one objection to the book is that the murderer goes unpunished by the law. However, it is obvious from the beginning that he is being punished daily by the mental anguish caused by his guilt. The tale has been very popular with girls from junior high up.

A booktalk about Rebecca is seldom necessary because the girls' own recommendations keep copies in circulation. However, a description of how the young couple met, pages 15–21; their growing friendship, 24–34, 36–45; his proposal of marriage when Mrs. Van Hopper has decided to take the girl to New York and she goes up to his room to say goodby, pages 51–56; and her meeting with Mrs. Danvers, pages 66–67, will rouse the interest of those who have not heard of the book.

My Cousin Rachel by DuMaurier tells of a woman who earned death by her dastardly conduct. Some young people will be interested in reading DuMaurier's *Myself When Young*, which tells how she struggled from her early years to become a writer and where she got some of her ideas for her novels and poetry. Other books that make good follow-ups to DuMaurier include Charlotte Bronte's *Jane Eyre*° and Emily Bronte's *Wuthering Heights*.

Embry, Joan

On Horses. 1984. Morrow.

Joan Embry summarizes her early years and interest in

animals, especially horses, and explains how she became a staff member at the San Diego Zoo and Wildlife Park. Her discussion of horses begins with the Przewalski, the wild Mongolian horse that is smaller than the domestic horse and is reddish with white markings on the head. Such horses may be extinct in the wild today, but a number of zoos and game farms breed them in captivity. She also describes the three types of zebras, each differently marked. Like the Przewalski, zebras do not make friends easily with humans. However, Joan has established a relationship with the young of these two families of horses, and she discusses their behavior briefly. She and her husband breed miniature horses on their ranch as well as Clydesdales and quarter horses. Part of her work at the zoo is training animals for the shows put on there; she also appears often on television with animals and has used various combinations of animals in her shows: zebras with horses and a camel with a horse, for example. She owns Leo, the horse used in the movie *Black Stallion*, and she often uses him. Stating that parades need a steady, patient animal, she tells the story of her first parade, when she rode an elephant and almost experienced a catastrophe. She briefly touches upon the three-day equestrian event that is a part of the Olympic Games and her participation in one. She has also trained and worked circus horses, but thinks circus life is too rigorous for her. Joan seems to want to be able to do all the jobs that can be done with horses; among her accomplishments are the ability to ride a cutting horse with a herd of cattle and to shoe a horse if she has to.

This very special book is liberally illustrated with outstanding color photographs by Robert Vavra, who wrote the introduction. Joan has a special empathy with animals because she loves them and is so knowledgeable about working with them.

The chapter on zebras, pages 22–29, and the one on miniature horses, pages 35, 76–79, could be used for booktalks. Charming photographs can be shown to the listeners.

If you are lucky enough to have a copy of the now out-of-print *My Wild World* by Embry, you can use it as a follow-up. She goes into much more detail here about her work at the zoo and includes many more kinds of animals. Phyllis Lose and Joan Embry have their love of horses in common. Each has made a different use of her ability to work with them. Lose's book is *No Job for a Lady.*°

Estey, Dale

A Lost Tale. 1980. St. Martin's.

The Isle of Man was settled originally by the Celts, and some of the Old Celtic customs and superstitions are still observed in the countryside. In this story, which takes place during World War II, Brigid Corvan and her mother, Fenella, both have the power and an inner vision. One moonlit night Brigid decides to go down to the beach, even though her father has told her that the German bombers will be flying and the excursion could be dangerous. As she nears the beach, she hears someone behind her and leads her pursuer a merry chase until suddenly he speaks to her. Though he is wearing a German uniform, he speaks English and says he is not a Nazi. She suddenly feels within herself that she can trust him. When they hear a bomber, he wants her to stay well back in the trees, but she tries to get to the beach. The bomber comes, circles, and comes back to drop a bomb. It circles again, and the soldier tries to force the pilot to drop the second bomb in the water by firing at the plane. The pilot fires back, and the soldier is hit. Brigid's father, who has come down to the beach with his rifle, takes aim at the German, but a white-maned head touches his arm and a long, spiral horn nudges the rifle aside. Here the reader learns that Brigid has been meeting a white unicorn at different times and places. Because the German has to be hidden and cared for until his wounds heal, the Head Druid finds a safe place for him and calls a meeting of the Druid Council. Taggart fears that Hitler is about to unleash some terrible destruction and hopes that the Druids can prevent it. The only female Druid has dreamed of a terrible holocaust—islands of fire, seas of flame, and many people dying in the cities. The youngest Druid, realizing he is being followed, tells Taggart, and the two of them find the stranger, who tells them that both Germany and England are working on an atomic bomb. He knows that the father of the young German is a scientist on a secret mission. The son, who is supposed to guide him across the island, has to choose between his fanatical Nazi father and his love for Brigid. With the help of the animals on the island, tragedy is averted.

This story of the supernatural, fairies, a unicorn, romance, meaningful dreams, and cooperative animals is convincingly written, and the characters are well drawn. Many teenage readers find the book delightful.

For a booktalk use the episode in which Brigid meets the man who is following her in the woods near the beach, the bomber comes, and the young man is shot, pages 3–21.

Those who enjoyed shivering over the supernatural events in which a young American girl at a small college in Wales plays a leading role (Dixie Tenny's *Call the Darkness Down*) can be introduced to *A Lost Tale.* In *Distant Summer* by Sarah Patterson, sixteen-year-old Kate Hamilton falls in love with an RAF rear gunner stationed nearby. As more and more planes are shot down during World War II, Kate suffers anguish. Will John come home safely? *The Listening Silence* by Marie Joseph concerns another young girl during World War II. She lives in England and is deaf and very skilled at lip reading. There is nothing supernatural in her story, but there is a nice romance.

Ford, Richard

Quest for the Faradawn. 1982. Delacorte/Eleanor Friede.

One Christmas Eve, Brock, a mature badger, watches an Urkku (human) couple enter Silver Wood and leave a blanketed infant at the base of a large oak tree. When they do not return, Brock approaches the child, who smiles and gurgles at him. He takes the baby home to his pregnant mate, Tara, who is able to feed the little human with her milk. A council, called the following night to inform the other animals living in Silver Wood, decides to allow the baby to stay with Brock. However, the Elflord has to be told, and Warrigal, a young owl, undertakes that task. Named Nab, the baby flourishes in his new home. By the time he is three, he is too big to live in the sett with the badgers, and they build him a home in nearby rhododendron bushes. In his eleventh year Nab first sees members of his own kind. Perryfoot (a brown hare), Brock, and Nab are on a walk when they see a little girl with her mother. They hide nearby, and while the woman is napping and the child picking flowers, Nab draws close to her. When she sees him, she speaks, but he cannot understand because he knows only the animals' language. That autumn, when Nab is walking with Rufus, two Urkku suddenly appear, shoot the fox, and capture Nab, whom their mother shuts in a second-floor bedroom after they reach home. In this house lives Sam, a golden-haired dog, who is friendly with the animals and keeps them informed about the Urkkus's plans. He carries the news of Nab's capture and is one of the animals involved in his dramatic rescue. The boy is soon sent on a journey with Brock to meet the Elflord, Lord Wychnor, who not only tells them the history of the elves and the Urkku but also explains what Nab is expected to do. Nab is given the Belt of Ammdar and a ring that he is to give the Lady of Eldron. On Christmas Eve the girl Nab had seen earlier looks out the window and sees him. She realizes she has to leave home quietly and join him. The remainder of the story tells of their journey with Brock, Warrigal, Sam, and Perryfoot and the dangers they encounter on their way to collect the three Faradawn from the Lords of the Seas, the Mountains, and the Woodlands in order to save the world from destruction.

The story is beautifully told, and the reader who enjoys fantasy can easily enter into the narrative and experience the joys, tragedies, and unusual adventures of the protagonists. The end comes suddenly and is a bit disappointing. The author's appended note explains it somewhat and possibly points to a sequel. Lovely drawings add to the enjoyment of the book.

Probably the best booktalk will tell of Brock's rescue of the baby and his gaining permission to keep Nab, in chapters 1–4.

Another fantasy in which an animal plays an important role is *The Woman Who Loved Reindeer* by Meredith Ann Pierce. Caribou's tribe live on the tundra, which is becoming turbulent because of earthquakes and volcanoes. Caribou is only twelve when her sister-in-law brings her a beautiful boy to care for. The boy's father can assume the body of either a stag or a man. When the boy is grown, he assumes the form of a stag to help Caribou lead her people to a safer land. *The Neverending Story* by Michael Ende is another fantasy about a young boy on a long trek. It is even more fantastic than Ford's. The author's imagination has produced some unusual scenery, characters, and events. Many young people will know the story because of the movie. In *Song of the Kingdom* Andy Stone describes the adventures of Orin, Tor, and Megan, three musicians, as they make the difficult journey to Star Peak, where the "Song of the Kingdom" had been buried when the kingdom fell into disunity and the playing of music had been forbidden.

Francis, Dick

The Danger. 1984. Putnam.

Liberty Market Ltd., made up mostly of ex-S.A.S., ex-police, and some who had done ultrasecret work in a government department, advises corporations and wealthy persons how to protect themselves from kidnappers. If a person should be kidnapped, Liberty works with the police on the case. Usually the person is returned safely, and often all or part of the ransom is recovered. Andrew Douglas, thirty and unmarried, is assigned to a case in Italy in which Alessia Cenci, a jockey and the daughter of a wealthy Italian businessman, is kidnapped. Andrew takes over the chauffeur's work in the Cenci household. One day when he is waiting for Cenci, who has a telephone rendezvous with the kidnapper, Andrew slumps behind the wheel to nap. A young man taps on the window and a conversation ensues. As the man turns away, Andrew realizes he has seen the man during an earlier case when the ransom has been paid and the police have unexpectedly attacked. Using modern technology Andrew creates a very good likeness of the man, to be used on Wanted posters. Eventually Andrew gets Alessia back, and the police arrest all the kidnappers but the leader. Andrew returns to his office in England, and Alessia goes to stay with a horsy friend near London. Andrew sees her quite often as she gradually recovers her desire to ride horses again. It is a quiet summer, but in August the three-year-old son of the owner of a winning horse is snatched. Andrew and another man are assigned to the case. Again they rescue the child and the police pick up all the kidnappers but the leader. Every year an international race is held at the Laural racecourse near Washington, D.C., and some of the super horses from Europe are invited. Alessia, who is again racing, is asked to ride one of the horses, and Morgan Freemantle, senior steward at the Jockey Club in England, is invited as guest of honor. On the second day of his visit, he is kidnapped. Andrew again takes on the case, but a few days after he arrives in Washington, he too is kidnapped. The reader learns how he eventually escapes and how Freemantle is found and the young leader of the kidnappers killed.

The method that Liberty Market Ltd. uses on a kidnapping case is very interesting, and the readers learn quite a bit about the psychology applied. The characters are interesting, the suspense is well sustained, and there is a bit of romantic interest. Those junior high readers who like mysteries read several of this author's books and enjoyed them.

Alessia's story of what the kidnappers did to her would make an interesting booktalk, pages 78–85.

The following novels by Francis can also be recommended. The problem in *Banker* concerns the reasons why the progeny of a famous stallion were born with defects. The young banker who had recommended making the loan for the purchase of the stallion almost loses his life in solving the mystery. Charles Todd in *In the Frame* finds that burglars have carried off his cousin's antique furniture, paintings, and other valuables; his cousin's wife has been murdered in the house; and his cousin is under suspicion. Young Philip Nore, whom we meet in *Reflex*, is a jockey. Because he is very interested in photography, he is instrumental in solving the supposedly accidental death of a well-known photographer of the horse-racing world. Although there is a great deal of information about the wine-making process, confirmed Francis fans will enjoy *Proof* in which a very likable young wine merchant helps snare several criminals who are funding a bottling plant where wine and whiskey are diluted and sold under false labels.

Frank, Anne

Anne Frank: The Diary of a Young Girl. 1952. Doubleday.

Anne Frank receives a diary for her thirteenth birthday on June 12, 1942, and because she has no close friend to whom she can confide her innermost thoughts, she decides to use her new diary for the purpose, calling her imaginary confidante "Kitty." Anne and her family have fled to Holland from Germany to escape Hitler's anti-Jewish campaign, and shortly after the Germans invade Holland, the family has to flee again. This time it is to a hiding place in an empty warehouse that Mr. Frank has been preparing for some time. Anne calls it "The Secret Annexe." They are joined shortly by the Van Daams— father, mother, and fifteen-year-old Peter. Besides confiding her secrets, the problems of growing up, and her difficulties with her mother, sister, and Mrs. Van Daam, Anne describes the characteristics and failings of the two families with girlish candor. The families are very restricted in their hiding place for over two years, but their lives are made bearable by Dutch friends who bring food, books, and other necessities, especially news. Since Anne wants to do something for these fine people, she saves for months the sugar she usually has on her porridge so that she can make fondants for them. One time their refuge is almost discovered when burglars break into the warehouse. Anne writes at that time, "If God lets me live, I shall attain more than Mummy ever has done. I shall not remain insignificant; I shall work in the world and for mankind." Anne and Peter are beginning to take a romantic interest in one another shortly before the families are discovered by the Gestapo. All but Mr. Frank die in a concentration camp two months before Holland is liberated by the Allies.

A very moving, revealing account of the feelings of a young girl growing up, this book is popular with readers from junior high up because they can imagine themselves in Anne's circumstances. It is useful as a teenage and family story and as a war and imprisonment tale.

For booktalks a brief summary is usually sufficient to interest readers, as most young people have heard of Anne Frank.

A juvenile book about Jewish young people during World War II could lead to the story of Anne Frank. *The Upstairs Room* by Johanna Reis tells the true experiences of a Dutch Jewish child hidden by a Dutch farm family. Follow up with *Anne Frank: A Portrait in Courage* by Ernst Schnabel, which adds information Anne did not give herself. *Field of Buttercups* by Joe Hyams tells how Dr. Janusz Korczak cared for Jewish children in the Warsaw ghetto when the Germans were exterminating the Jews as fast as they could. *A Square of Sky* by Janina David opens in 1939 when the author was nine years of age and living in Poland with her comfortably situated Jewish family. She describes the terrors and deprivations of life in the

Warsaw ghetto until her parents make possible her escape after four years. Please refer to the entry on Kitty Hart for other books about Jewish young people of that period. A natural follow-up to Anne Frank's *Diary* is *Anne Frank Remembered: The Story of Miep Gies, Who Helped to Hide the Frank Family,*° a touching memoir by Miep Gies with Alison Leslie Gold.

Fuller, Elizabeth

Nima: A Sherpa in Connecticut. 1984. Dodd, Mead.

John G. Fuller and his wife Elizabeth are both writers. In 1980 they decided to take time out of their busy lives to visit Nepal in the Himalayas for a forty-day trek toward Mount Everest. Their constant companion and guide was a teenage Sherpa named Nima, who really took good care of them. When they discovered he had tuberculosis, they were more than amazed that he could carry heavy loads. As the days passed, he became thinner and frailer. When they were about to board their plane to return to the United States, they asked him if he would like to visit them in their home in Connecticut. Six months passed before Nima, just a shadow of his former self, came to the United States. Immediately Elizabeth made a doctor's appointment for him, and the young man spent several days in the hospital for tests and treatment. The doctor said the boy was gravely ill but would fully recover with medication, proper food, and lots of rest, and he did. The author relates episodes from their trip to Nepal as the family's daily activities in the United States reminded her of them. She also tells of Nima's adjusting to life in America. He was introduced to TV during his long rest periods, and Fuller describes several humorous events. As he gained weight and strength, Nima was allowed to ride a bike and explore, go shopping with his hostess, and meet family friends. The Fullers had decided to get a new roof put on their house and add another room to the second floor. A man who became one of Nima's dearest friends headed the construction crew and did the remodeling. There are many entertaining episodes as Nima learned to use carpentry tools and helped on the construction. Eventually he went to night school to improve his English, and he took first aid classes. When his year in the States was up, it was difficult to say good-bye. Nima had saved quite a sum of money from his allowance and the money the contractor paid him, and he was looking forward to being able to build his own teahouse when he reached home.

Nima is a delightful person. The reader gets a good idea of the Sherpas' religious views and their philosophy of life. The account is entertaining and often touching. Nima's visit was not easy for the Fullers in some ways, and we have to admire their ability to cope with the boy's effervescence and enthusiasm.

A booktalk can be built from tiny episodes in chapter 1 when Nima first arrived for his visit to the Fullers. Another possibility is Nima's reaction to advertising on TV, pages 50–52. These endear the boy to the reader.

Fuller, John G.

The Day We Bombed Utah: America's Most Lethal Secret. 1984. New American Library.

In 1951 the Atomic Energy Commission (AEC) began atomic testing only a few miles from Bullochs' ranch, a lead mine, and several small towns in Utah. Government men warned the mine owner that the mine should be shut down during a test. They also said that families should be evacuated from the area at these times, even though they claimed the fallout would be below the danger level. As time went on, the blasts became more powerful, and winds blew the fallout over the populated areas. In March 1953, Fern and Mac Bulloch began to drive their flocks from winter range toward home. When they reached the ranch, the sheep began to die, and lambs were born badly deformed or dead. The wool of adult sheep came off in chunks and had changed in consistency. Other owners of flocks experienced similar tragedy. Together owners lost 4,390 sheep, suffering financial disaster. The residents of St. George, a town of about five thousand, had received a concentration of beta rays thirty-three times that of most areas in Utah. Horses and cattle in Nevada and Utah had beta burns. Some appeared to be blinded; others were dead. Veterinarians found that a radiation meter used on the dead sheep went off the upper end of the scale. The AEC sent investigators, who claimed the radiation was not high enough to seriously affect the sheep. They said the trouble was malnutrition without a doubt. Thus began the AEC's cover-up efforts, and the testing of weapons continued. The veterinarians who blamed the deaths on radiation were coerced into changing their testimony. When the RKO film company wanted to make a film in the area, it was allowed. Years later the four stars, the producer, and almost half the cast and crew died of cancer. When an unusual number of people in St. George began to die of cancer or leukemia, the AEC again hid evidence pointing at nuclear testing as the cause. Underground testing did not lessen the danger because the deadly materials usually found a vent through which to escape into the atmosphere. The United States is not the only country carrying on such experiments. The author says the American, Soviet, French, British, and Chinese brands of iodine-131, cesium-137, and strontium-90 form a common enemy against all the people of the world.

Because of congressional subpoenas and the Freedom of Information Act, documents hidden by the AEC and the Department of Energy over the years have been released. From this information and interviews with people living and working in Utah and Nevada, the author was able to get the information for his book. It is a chilling exposé.

Some details about what happened to the Bulloch brothers' sheep may interest readers in finding out the facts about how the United States government is killing its citizens in peacetime with nuclear weapons.

Another example of how the U.S. government has knowingly failed to protect some of its citizens may be found in *Kerry: Agent Orange and an American Family* by Clifford Linedecker with Michael and Maureen Ryan. Michael was a soldier in Vietnam stationed in an area heavily sprayed with Agent Orange and other defoliants. As a result he suffered many ills; Kerry, his only child, had twenty-two abnormalities at birth and will always be handicapped. In *Bill Kurtis on Assignment* the reporter describes the veterans he interviewed in order to learn of their experiences with Agent Orange, what he and his team observed in Vietnam, and the use of herbicides on farms in the United States. In *Waiting for an Army to Die: The Tragedy of Agent Orange*, Fred A. Wilcox has documented cases of a number of Vietnam veterans who are suffering or have died from the effects of Agent Orange. He includes cases of miscarriages by women exposed to spraying of trees near their homes, and he quotes doctors who testify that accidental release of dioxin and other chemicals in several countries has caused cancer in people exposed to them. He also covers the findings of attorneys bringing suits against chemical companies.

Gaan, Margaret

Little Sister. 1983. Dodd, Mead.

A successful businessman in Shanghai, John Erle Lancy, an American with a Chinese wife, has a large home and grounds. At the time of the story, 1925, Little Sister, the child of the Lancy's third son, is an alert six-year-old. Grandfather has written that he wants Little Sister to attend the English school in Shanghai. Seventeen-year-old Celia, daughter of the first son, is already living at her grandparents' home to have special English lessons. She and Little Sister share a room and love one another dearly. Lik, a son adopted by the Lancys as a baby, still lives at home; he and Min-Li, son of one of the servants, have grown up together. Now at age twenty-one they are working men and members of the Communist party. Because conditions in the factories, many owned by foreigners, are dreadful and wages minimal, the communists are planning a citywide strike and a protest march. Lik, who is one of the leaders, is wounded when the British set up barricades and, at one point, open fire. When word reaches home, only Grandmother, who doesn't speak English, and Little Sister are there. Calling for her ricksha, Grandmother goes to the American Embassy, taking Little Sister with her as interpreter. There Grandmother shows documents that prove Lik is an American, and the embassy official takes Grandmother and Little Sister to the police station, where he demands Lik's release. In this way Lik finds out who his real parents are; he and Celia, who have fallen in love and plan to marry, have the same father. Now the marriage, of course, is impossible. When Celia finds out and learns of Lik's departure with Min-li to Canton, she decides to commit suicide, but Little Sister saves her.

So much love is expressed in this family, and most members

have such a wonderful sense of humor, that readers can't help but empathize with them. Gann obviously understands the way children's minds work, and her delineation of Little Sister is especially fine. Grandmother, Grandfather, and Celia are also well drawn. The frequent humorous experiences so evocative of a large but close family are often the result of something Little Sister did or said. The author herself grew up in just such a home in Shanghai with an American grandfather and Chinese grandmother. Readers will learn a little Chinese political history very painlessly.

A booktalk could include the incident when Grandmother purchases baby ducks to raise and fatten for the family table. Little Sister and her cousin Carrie decide to help fatten the ducks by feeding them some nice fat worms they have found, but by the time the girls reach the ducks, half the worms have crawled out of the container. As a result of Little Sister's bright idea to keep the worms quiet, all the ducks die. Her voluntary confession and explanation to her grandparents are hilarious, pages 5–11. Min-li's trial shows how badly the Chinese were treated in their own country by foreigners, pages 56–63.

Homesick, My Own Story by Jean Fritz is a juvenile book about the author's early years in China where her father had charge of the YMCA at Hankow. Good readers who enjoyed the charming autobiography can be introduced to *Little Sister.* Margaret Gaan's *Last Moments of a World* describes her own family's experiences under the Japanese occupation of China and the struggle between the forces of Generalissimo Chiang Kai-shek and those of Mao Tse-tung. Readers will find more information about the cultural revolution in China in *In the Eye of the Typhoon* by Ruth Lo and Katharine Kinderman. Mrs. Lo was an American married to a Chinese professor; their two children in their twenties played leading roles in helping their parents endure persecution by the Red Guards. *Second Daughter: Growing up in China, 1930–1949* by Katherine Wei and Terry Quinn tells of another Chinese family with similar political and economic problems. Katherine's brilliance and independent thinking as a child and teenager make this story especially appealing. Another very nice story (nonpolitical) of a little Chinese girl is *One of the Lucky Ones*° by Lucy Ching. See page 21.

Gann, Ernest K.

The Aviator.   1981.   Arbor House.

In *Mayday! Mayday!* by Hilary Milton, eleven-year-old Allison and fourteen-year-old Mark are the least injured of the two families aboard a light plane that encountered a bad weather front and crashed on the side of an Alabama mountain after dark. The young people meet numerous obstacles as they try to walk for help. Those who want an adult story should be introduced to Heather in *The Aviator.* Jerry was badly injured when one of his students crashed their training plane. He mended after a stay in the hospital, but doctors could do nothing about the scarred and scorched side of his face. No one wanted to hire him, but Jerry finally found a job in Elko, Nevada, flying the mail to Boise, Idaho, and one winter day he also carried a passenger, eleven-year-old Heather. When the plane's engine fails, Jerry has to land on a mountainside, where the plane is torn apart by trees. Although both pilot and passenger survive, Heather is badly injured. Jerry has a chocolate bar, a bottle of ten pain pills, a gun, and a few tools. He manages to build a shelter to protect them from the falling snow, but there are no animals around to be killed for food. He builds a fire to melt snow for a pine-needle tea and finds a way to take care of Heather's physical needs. On the first day after the crash Jerry invents a game to help the girl cope with the pain between medication, and he gives her letters to read from the mailbags. On the second day one letter is from a young woman whose husband of two years has been killed in a bad accident. Both Jerry and Heather have to respect the woman's attitude about love and her husband's sudden death. That letter and his admiration for Heather make Jerry realize that his eight years of isolation since his disfigurement have been the wrong way to handle his problem, and he decides to try to get them off the mountain before his strength fails. Because of Heather's back injury, he can't carry her without some support; she will have to sit on a seat. Gritting her teeth, she lets him gradually sit her up. Because the weather has turned warm, causing avalanches, he has to be very careful going down the mountain. It is a grueling trip, but they eventually reach safety.

The simple story, well told, is not just of survival but of the struggle of a man who has been unable to face and overcome his handicap. Heather is a strong character whom readers—both boys and girls—will admire.

A true story of survival of an airplane crash is *The Sacrament* by Peter Gzowski. Some members of a Canadian family flying from their hometown to Boise, Idaho, go down in a storm. After recuperating from severe injuries for two weeks and having to eat part of the body of another family member, teenage Donna and her brother-in-law are finally able to walk out to a settlement. In another true story, *And I Alone Survived*, Lauren Elder tells of her difficulty in getting back to civilization after the plane in which she was riding crashed, killing the pilot and the other passenger. In Jack Rowe's *Inyo-Sierra Passage*, Jack Laird (who buys, repairs, and sells damaged aircraft) hires Jim Regan, a promising young pilot, to fly an eight-seat, executive twin-engine plane from Southern California to Reno, Nevada. Expecting to make a small fortune off the plane's insurance, Jack makes sure the plane will crash by tampering with several parts of its mechanism. Jim survives, cared for by an old Indian woman who saw the plane crash, but he isn't found for over a month.

Gies, Miep, and Alison Leslie Gold

Anne Frank Remembered. 1987.
Simon & Schuster.

As a young woman Miep Gies helps the Frank family when they are hiding from the Nazis during World War II. Born in Vienna, Austria, a few years before World War I, Miep is small and not very strong, and because of serious food shortages during the war, she is undernourished and sick. In 1920 she and many other Austrian children are sent to the Netherlands to be revitalized. Miep is ten and speaks only German. She is entered immediately into school and by spring is the best student in her class. She should have returned to her family at the end of three months, but the doctors keep extending her time because she is still weak. When she is sixteen, the Dutch family takes her back to Vienna, but it is obvious she will not be happy there. Her blood relatives do not seem like family, and so she returns to Amsterdam. When she finishes school, she hears of an opening at Travies and Company; she applies and is hired, thus meeting Otto Frank, Anne's father, who soon moves his family from Germany to the Netherlands. Miep meets Anne, who is only four, and the two take to one another immediately. More and more Jews are seeking refuge in Holland; in 1938 hundreds of Jewish businesses and synagogues are smashed and burned in Germany. The German army invades Austria and then Poland, Denmark, Norway, and finally, Holland. In the spring of 1942 the Frank family goes into hiding, and Miep agrees to care for their needs. Although her own life is constantly in danger, Miep never hesitates to do what she has to do to keep the refugees fed and to provide rare goodies to make their closely confined lives more bearable. Eventually they are discovered and taken away. Miep's love story and marriage are included in the book. Holland is a very crowded country, and one marvels at the conditions under which Miep and Henk have to live. After the war Mr. Frank lives with them for several years.

Anyone who has read Anne Frank's story will want to read Miep's, too. She was an ingenious, brave young woman, and her life story is interesting and well worth reading. She and Anne were particularly close, and Miep's account adds dimension to Anne's book.

The moving of the Franks into their hiding place is described in pages 82–86 and could be used for a booktalk if one is needed.

For other stories about Jewish people in World War II see Frank, Anne, *Anne Frank: Diary of a Young Girl.*° In 1944 Raoul Wallenberg was sent by the Swedish government to Hungary to try to rescue the Jews destined for German concentration camps. This young man's great personal authority and caring so amazed the SS men and Hungarian Fascists that he was able to save thousands of Jews from the death camps. His story is told by John Bierman in *Righteous Gentile.* Another instance of opposition to Hitler's regime is found in *Students against Tyranny* by Inge Scholl, a sister of two young Germans, both students at the University of Munich, who tried to arouse young people to passive resistance to the Nazis and were executed early in 1943. In *The Hiding Place*, Corie Ten Boom, a Dutch writer, tells how she helped many Jews to safety during the war. Very good readers will love Philip Hallie's *Lest Innocent Blood Be Shed.* He tells of the love for humanity and the courage of Andre Troome, pastor of the

Protestant church in the small French village of Le Chambon and of the other villagers and the farmers in the surrounding area who provided shelter for hundreds of Jews fleeing from the Germans during World War II. In *Walls: Resisting the Third Reich*, Hiltgunt Zassenhaus, a young German woman, describes how she was able to help many political prisoners, mostly Scandinavians, in Germany during the war.

Godden, Rumer

The Dark Horse. 1981. Viking.

A two-year-old, Dark Invader won his first race at Lingfield in England, and since then has never been a winner. So it is not surprising when his owner accepts an offer for him from Mr. Leventine from Calcutta. The new owner insists that Dark Invader's stablehand, Ted Mullins, accompany the horse to India, all expenses paid. In Calcutta Mr. Leventine's horses are kept and trained at stables up the road from the convent run by the Sisters of Poverty, who have taken in some two hundred poor old men and women. To feed them, an old horse and wagon, loaded with big canisters, make the rounds of the restaurants late at night to collect the leftover food. Mother Morag, head of the convent, does not know how long the old horse will last or what they will do without him. When Ted and Dark Invader arrive, Mr. Leventine asks Ted to stay on in India. At one time Ted had been a jockey, and he begins to ride again, as the horse has its own Indian stablehands. The stable owner and his wife have several quite wild children known at the stables as the "bandar-log," the monkey people. The youngsters soon become very fond of Ted, who in turn likes them and is able to discipline them. About a week before Dark Invader's first race, the stable owner has to be away for a day, leaving Ted in charge. Unfortunately he gets hold of a couple bottles of whiskey and becomes drunk, and an immature jockey lets a visiting English jockey exercise Dark Invader. The horse throws the man, runs away, and cannot be found. The nuns' old horse has died suddenly, and Dark Invader takes refuge in his stall. Mother Morag announces that Dark Invader has come for sanctuary, and she will not give him up. It takes several days of negotiating before the horse is returned, and Mother Morag has a new wagon and young horse in exchange—all paid for by Mr. Leventine.

Although the horse is the protagonist of the story, it is not the most important participant. There are several well-drawn, likable characters. Humorous moments add much to the story. The care lavished on the horses is quite a contrast to the extreme poverty and wretched living conditions of the common people of India.

When the stable owner needs to expand, he offers to buy the convent and its outbuildings; Mother Morag explains why she cannot sell, pages 8–11. Pages 11–17 tell about the good deeds of the nuns and how hard they have to work. Pages 51–59 describe Ted and Dark Invader's first experience in Calcutta. Pages 95–97 show how Ted trained the "bandar-log."

In another horse story, high school senior Mike Benson spots a big gray horse in a horse dealer's paddock during Easter vacation. He is drawn to it in spite of its poor condition and buys it with all the savings he has. With proper care the horse blossoms, and after many difficulties Mike rides it in a sensational race. Any boy or girl who was thrilled by reading *A Horse to Remember* by Sam Savitt will enjoy this adult novel, *A Dark Horse. On Horses*° by Joan Embry is not about racing, but it will interest those who are enthusiastic about horses. Because *International Velvet* by Bryan Forbes was published in 1978, younger readers may have missed it. It is a nice sequel to *National Velvet* by Enid Bagnold and teaches some valuable lessons.

Godden, Rumer

Thursday's Children.   1984.   Viking.

Ma danced in a chorus line before she married Pa Penny, and her dearest wish is to have a daughter who will become a ballerina. But they have four boys before a baby girl arrives; she is named Crystal. The last baby, Doone, is a surprise and not really welcomed by the family because there is no room for him. Crystal, of course, takes dancing lessons, and because she has to look after Doone, he accompanies her to class three days a week. Fascinated by the work the girls do at the barre and by their arm work in the center of the room, Doone is soon going out into the hall, holding on to the radiator and doing the same exercises. He also plays on his mouth organ the music old Mr. Felix plays on the piano. Ma insists that the class be entered in a competition with other schools of dance, and when one of the children is withdrawn at the last minute, Mr. Felix suggests that Doone take her place. The six-year-old boy makes a hit with the audience and judges; Crystal is the only one not commended for her dancing. Blaming the teachers, Ma insists that Crystal go to another school. The new teacher is so interested in Doone that she gives him free lessons. Crystal works hard here and is eventually selected to attend Queen's Chase, the Junior School of Her Majesty's Ballet. In a couple of years Doone is also admitted. Jealous of the attention some of the girls and Doone receive, Crystal plays some dirty tricks on them. She dances well but is not as outstanding as she might have been. Yuri Koszora, a young male dancer who is a star at the Royal Theatre, comes to the school when Crystal is in her next-to-last year and designs a new ballet for the Junior School. Crystal is one of the four girls chosen for a part. All of them do well, but it is Doone who makes headlines by being chosen to take the part of Yuri as a child in a TV show. As the story unfolds both children seem destined to be stars in the future.

This is not only a delightful story of ballet but also a moving family tale. The characters are very well drawn, and Doone especially is a charming child. Crystal, very jealous of Doone after his first successful performance, finally learns to live with and rejoice at his accomplishments.

The episode when Doone, at age six, substitutes in a harlequinade as a clown, delighting the whole audience, would make an interesting booktalk if a bit about the little boy's background is included, pages 18–19, 24–25, 34–36.

Young people who enjoyed *Worlds Apart*, the autobiography of Robert Maiorano, soloist with the New York City Ballet, will like reading Godden's novel about another boy who became a dancer. *The Dancers of Sycamore Street* by Julie L'Enfant is another adult story of young dancers. These are from Mme. Le Breton's advanced class, which is chosen to present a new ballet by the artistic director of the National Dance Theatre. *A Company of Swans* by Eva Ibbotson is a bit sophisticated for younger girls in junior high, but the more advanced ninth-grade readers will love it. It tells of an eighteen-year-old girl in England who runs away from a very repressive home life to join a Russian ballet company that will tour South America. It has a nice romance that ends properly but, for a time, includes some premarital sex. When Merrill Ashley was fourteen she began her ballet training under choreographer George Balanchine and worked for him for sixteen years. She tells about those years and how much they meant to her in *Dancing for Balanchine* and also demonstrates various positions, movements, and basic ballet steps in sequence photographs. The book is recommended for ballet enthusiasts and students as well as for young persons fortunate enough to see professional ballet performances. In *Leap Year* Christopher D'Amboise describes the year after he finished high school, when he was invited to join the New York City Ballet. He meditates on his future, friendships, some authors he has read, and women. Wendy Neale, who wrote *Ballet Life behind the Scenes,* is not a dancer, but she has talked with many performers with the American Ballet Theatre and the New York City Ballet and often includes their words as she discusses classes, rehearsals, performances, working with choreographers, injuries, diet, and health.

Gooden, Dwight, with *Richard Woodley*

Rookie.   1985.   Doubleday.

The New York Mets' star pitcher, Dwight Gooden, is chosen as National League Rookie of the Year in 1984. He is only nineteen, but he has set a number of records during that baseball season. He appears to be fairly modest, admitting some of his weaknesses on the playing field and, matter-of-factly, his accomplishments. He grows up in Tampa, Florida, where he plays Little League baseball. He pitches some but also plays third base and the outfield and is a good hitter. He is fortunate to have a good coach who forces him to use all his talent. He develops a very good fastball pitch and curve ball. An average student in high school, he decides that if he is not drafted by a major league team after he graduates, he will attend college. In 1982 his name is number five in the first round draft, and he is chosen by the Mets. At seventeen he leaves home to play in the Appalachian League, earning $600 a month. A former teammate, who had spent his senior year in California, is also drafted by the Mets, and this makes Gooden's first year away from home a bit easier. He plays well and in August is sent up to Little Falls in a higher league. In 1983 he moves up to the Class A South Atlantic League. In 1984 he spends spring training with the New York Mets and, at the end of that period, is told he will be one of the team's four starting pitchers. From here on he gives the details about the games he pitches and tells how carefully he is handled so that he will not overdo and injure himself. He is chosen to pitch in the All-Star game, and in his two innings he strikes out three and gives up only one hit.

Baseball fans will enjoy the book and will certainly remember seeing Gooden play. He is a good example of how a rookie should conduct himself and how a young player should be handled. The writing is better than that of most books by athletes.

It is probably not necessary to use an incident from the book in talking about it. A mention of the title and author or a summary similar to the one above should sell the book to sports fans.

A baseball enthusiast will get a lot of joy out of reading *The Artful Dodger* by Tommy Lasorda, known as baseball's Goodwill Ambassador. This autobiography is laugh provoking, inspiring, outlandish, deeply moving, and well worth reading. Another story of a phenomenal young athlete is *Kurt Thomas on Gymnastics* by Kurt Thomas and Kent Hannon. Until Thomas became an international star, few people even knew what gymnastics were. Besides describing Kurt's career up to 1980, the book gives information on training, gymnasts from other countries, watching a meet, judging, and the history of gymnastics. Sports fans will also enjoy reading *One Goal* by John Powers and Arthur C. Kaminsky, which tells about the building of the 1980 U.S. Olympic hockey team and of its winning the gold medal. Some young pro football fans will enjoy reading *Rosey: The Gentle Giant* by Roosevelt Grier, an unusual, loving person. He describes briefly almost every game he played, and while some of this narrative can be skipped if necessary, readers should not miss his references to his philosophy of life. His work after retirement with inner-city teens and for senior citizens as well as his acceptance of religion as an essential part of his life add an important dimension to his story.

Graham, Robin Lee, and *Hill, Derek*

Home Is the Sailor. 1983. Harper.

This sequel to *Dove* continues the story of Robin Lee Graham and his wife Patti, a California girl he meets in the Fiji Islands on his voyage alone around the world in a small boat. She does not travel with him but meets him later in Durban, South Africa, where they marry; however, they are not truly united until he finally reaches Los Angeles. Soon their first child is born. In the South Pacific the young couple talked of homesteading in Canada. Before they make up their minds, Robin is offered a full scholarship at Stanford University, but he drops out before the end of the first semester. Just after the New Year, a writer approaches Robin and suggests they collaborate on a book about Robin's solo voyage. At about the same time, religion becomes an important part of Robin and Patti's lives, and when the book *Dove* is finished, Robin and his family settle in Kalispel, Montana, where they buy land on a mountain outside of town and build a cabin. Though they love the area, they have no adequate income and, because of their inexperience, cannot make a living off the land. Eventually, when the boat *Dove* is sold and the book published, some money comes in, but they soon spend it on more land, more equipment, and better transportation. All during these months their Christian faith has been growing, and they have many experiences for which they thank God. The success of the book brings a movie offer. The way this comes about makes a very interesting part of their story. However, all is not happiness and light. Robin tends to be moody when everything does not go right, and the reader has to admire Patti for the way she handles this situation. Eventually the young couple finds solutions to their problems.

The joy and love of the young couple and their little daughter are heartwarming. Young readers will find inspiration in the story, and it should make them realize how difficult life can be when a young father lacks education and training. Eventually Robin finds work for which he is suited, but until that time he is fortunate to have some income from the book and movie. Passages from Patti's journal which are quoted add a great deal.

Patti and Robin's arrival in Kalispel and their finding a place to live would make an interesting booktalk after introducing the characters, pages 46–50. Robin's encounters with a black bear, pages 71–72, and their early experiences after they move into the cabin are alternatives, pages 78–84.

Although *Joy in the Morning* by Betty Smith and *Mr. and Mrs. Bo Jo Jones* by Anne Head consider the problems arising in only the first year of marriage, young readers have liked these books very much, and they are still in print. They can be recommended as follow-up titles. Some readers will want to read *Dove*, in which Robin tells of his experiences on his leisurely trip around the world.

Green, Wayne L.

Allegiance. 1983. Crown.

In 1943 the Japanese held Attu, the westernmost of the Aleutians. In its effort to wrest the island from the enemy the United States sent troops, the Navy, and land-based planes. This story concerns a young Navy fighter pilot, Michael Andrews, whose plane is shot down over Attu. Mike is wounded and has burns across his back, but he manages to land in a snowy valley and get out before the plane explodes. After eluding the Japanese for a short time, he is captured and taken to the field hospital area. He is so covered with mud that his rescuers do not realize he is an American. When Dr. Tomi Nakamura is examining him, Mike whispers, "Don't let me die." Tomi has only seconds to make up his mind. His duty is to the emperor, but Tomi is a Christian; he lived in the United States for nine years while in medical school and he liked the Americans. He had not wanted to join the Japanese army but had been drafted. After washing Mike and caring for his wounds, he shrouds him from head-top to waistline in white bandages as he would a burn case. There are four threads in the story: Tomi's attempt to save Mike; Mike's recall of friendship with his girl; the American attacks, particularly those of the Third Squad under Sgt. John Murphy, which kill more and more Japanese and force the survivors to retreat to a small area; and finally the activities in the field hospital, where the wounded are brought in, patched up, and often sent back to fight. Finally, the Japanese plan one last attack. If it fails, those who survive will kill themselves. Prepared by Tomi for his escape, Mike gets away. The American forces are not far away, and he reaches them safely, even though his weakness makes the trek difficult. Tomi stays at the hospital while all the workers there go to the front. When Mike reaches his compatriots, he insists that they try to rescue Dr. Nakamura. They find him, but by a fluke he is killed.

This is a very compelling, well-told story with some excellent characterizations. In conversations there are but a few objectionable words or sexual remarks. Even the girls in my group highly recommended this story.

Any of the following incidents can be used in a booktalk. After he crash lands, Mike finds a cave that the Japanese are using as a warehouse, and he hides there under a pile of clothes for a short time, pages 27–28, 35–37. Mike and Tomi Nakamura meet, and the doctor decides to help Mike, pages 38–44. Tomi and Mike have a chance to get acquainted, pages 60–62.

Also suggest *Deliverance at Los Bandos*, in which Anthony Arthur tells of the 2,147 civilian internees, adults and children, who survive the inadequate food and shelter provided by the Japanese in the Philippines during World War II. After three years the U.S. Army stages a dramatic rescue just hours before all the prisoners are to be liquidated. Manny Lawton was a captain in the U.S. Army stationed in the Philippines in 1942 when the Japanese invaded and within a short time forced the Americans to surrender. In *Some Survived* he tells of the terrible conditions he and others experienced as prisoners for more than three years.

Greenbaum, Dorothy, and *Laiken, Diedre S.*

Lovestrong: A Woman Doctor's True Story of Marriage and Medicine. 1984. Times.

Since the parents of Dorothy Fink and Eddie Greenbaum are friends, the two children play together when they are small, but in their teens they grow a little apart. Dorothy realizes she loves Eddie when she is in college preparing to become a high school English teacher, but it isn't until Eddie sees her as maid of honor at a cousin's wedding that he realizes she is the girl he wants. They are married in 1969, and both hold teaching positions. In 1971 their first child is born. Eddie is content with teaching in junior high school, but Dorothy finds the work is not challenging enough for her. When she finally decides she wants to become a doctor, Eddie says that if it will make her happy, he will help all he can. Her college work had included few pre-med credits. Thus she will have to take all the preparatory work and get straight A's if she is to enter medical school. That means taking time from family and housework for many hours of serious study. Eddie is not adept at housekeeping, and Dorothy's first response to a littered apartment and messy kitchen does not ease the situation. But these young people are really in love, and Eddie has promised to stand behind his wife's decision. Dorothy has to shrug her shoulders and accept the situation about housework. What does an accumulation of dust matter in the long run? Fortunately, her parents are able to take care of their child during Eddie's working hours. Dorothy describes her classes, some fellow students and their problems, her experiences while working in various hospitals, and their troubles when Eddie is laid off because of the city's budget crunch. No matter what happens, their love helps to carry them through their darkest hours. It takes ten years before Dorothy becomes a practicing pediatrician.

This true story has much to recommend it. The young couple's willingness to try to understand what each is experiencing and to find a way to help each other is heartwarming. Eddie's confidence in Dorothy's ability to conquer every obstacle—calculus, anatomy, thirty-six hour stints—gives her the impetus she needs. Dorothy's sincere wish to aid each patient and to carefully diagnose each illness is a contrast to the snap judgments and callousness of a few of her colleagues. The book gives young people a gauge against which to measure their own loves.

It is not easy to get into medical school; Dorothy tells of the struggle she had in pages 73–83. After Eddie loses his job, times are difficult. Pages 187–94 tell of some of the problems they have to face.

Although *The Flying Flynns* by Bethine Flynn is concerned with the author's work with her veterinarian husband, the emphasis is on their devotion to one another, the beauty of the western coast of Canada, and the friendliness of all the people they meet as they fly from one settlement to another. Another story of a successful marriage is *Cry of the Kalahari*° by Mark and Delia Owens. Here the young couple are in the same kind of work, which can sometimes lead to misunderstandings and jealousy but not with these people. They complement each other perfectly and thus are able to accomplish much. Another example of a couple who put their marriage first and work diligently to make it a success under what many would consider very difficult conditions is found in *Ruffles on my Longjohns* by Isabel Edwards. She and Earle lived on a homestead in British Columbia for almost fifty years beginning in 1932.

Griffin, John Howard

Black Like Me. 1961. 1977. Houghton.

In an effort to learn what life is really like for a black in the South, John Griffin disguises himself as a black and lives and travels for three months in Louisiana, Mississippi, and Alabama. An oral medication, given him by a dermatologist, and exposure to ultraviolet rays help to darken his skin. When he completes his makeup by using a stain and shaving his head, he does not recognize himself in a mirror. It is not difficult for him to make the transition because a black shoeshiner in whom he confides coaches him as they work, eat, and lounge together. Griffin finds white people and black equally courteous in giving him directions, but he has to follow the Jim Crow regulations in restrooms, restaurants, hotels, and the like. Wanting to see what chance an educated black man has of getting a decent job, he begins to look for work but has no luck. Only menial jobs are open. Occasionally he has opportunities to discuss the racial situation in the South with blacks who do not know he is white, and they talk freely, something they seldom do with white people. He tells of traveling by bus and hitchhiking. At times the hatred, injustice, insults, and fear he experiences nauseate him. When he can stand it no longer, he is forced to contact a white person he knows will be sympathetic, so that he can take a breather. He tells of many "incredible" (his word) kindnesses done for him by blacks who do not know his real identity, and he feels that in this way they compensate somewhat to one another for the degradation they suffer from whites. He explains how white people who say they regard the black as a brother often demonstrate their insincerity by certain words they use, stereotypes they believe in, and the superiority they obviously feel. Griffin does acknowledge that some white people in the South are decent and that in some ways progress is being made. The original book has not been changed, but an added epilogue in the 1977 edition briefly acknowledges some of the changes that have taken place since the book's original publication. Griffin has frequently been called upon by both whites and blacks to help in difficult racial situations.

While reading this, idealistic teenagers become black just as the author did, and through Griffin's eyes they experience the same shock and fear as Griffin begins to understand what blacks face daily.

The author has not omitted all the rough language and epithets used by whites and blacks. Experiences regarding sex are included to negate stereotyped ideas concerning blacks and to show how whites have abused blacks sexually. Because this was written between 1959 and 1961, Griffin used the word *Negro* rather than *black.* My group thought all teens should read this book.

A few brief statements telling the purpose of the author's trip through the South and how he made the transition from white to black may be enough to interest readers. The incident in which Griffin is befriended by a young black who lives with his wife and six children in a two-room shack in the woods, described on pages 113–23, could be worked into a booktalk.

For other books concerning the racial situation, suggest *Coming of Age in Mississippi,* in which black Anne Moody tells of her life in the Deep South from 1940 to 1964. Born in 1933, Mary Mebane grew up on a small farm in Durham County, North Carolina. In her autobiography, *Mary,*° she tells of poverty, lack of job opportunities, and inferior educational facilities. Fortunately she is able to rise above these difficulties. Chet Fuller, a prize-winning black reporter for the Atlanta *Journal,* is sent on an assignment to learn whether or not the civil rights movement in the South has had a real effect on black citizens. In *I Hear Them Calling My Name* he tells of the extreme poverty, scarcity of jobs, and lack of opportunities with which blacks have been confronted in recent years. Conditions had not changed since Griffin made a similar trip more than twenty years earlier.

Harrison, Harry

Make Room! Make Room! 1979.
Gregg. (1966. Doubleday.)

On August 9, 1999, there are 35 million people living in New York City. A long drought has limited food and water supplies. People are housed in mothballed ships, cars in parking lots, warehouses, tents, hallways, and on stairs, and some even live on the streets. Only a few people have money, luxurious apartments, and beautiful clothing. Billy Ching, a young Chinese boy who works as a Western Union messenger, sees how people with money live when he delivers a telegram to Michael O'Brien. Though the entrance to the building is closely guarded, Billy notices that the burglar alarm at O'Brien's door has been disconnected. As he is leaving, he goes down to the basement to find another way into the building and sees a side window with a disconnected burglar alarm. Then he leaves by the front entrance. The next morning O'Brien's mistress rises early, picks up her bodyguard at the entrance, and goes shopping. While they are gone, Billy forces open the basement window with a sharpened tire iron and enters; next he forces the door to O'Brien's apartment. Seeing no one in the rooms, he begins to go through the drawers in the bedroom. Suddenly the bathroom door opens and O'Brien walks out. Billy lashes out with the tire iron, O'Brien drops, and the boy flees. The fingerprints on the iron cannot be identified by the police. Andy Rusch is permanently assigned to the case although he still has to put in his usual hours on patrol. The author follows Billy's desperate efforts to find a safe hiding place and some way to get food and water. Andy, investigating everyone who has made deliveries to the apartment house, eventually arrests Billy.

The novel graphically depicts the horrific effects of overpopulation on a city and a country. The United States government is presented in a very unflattering light; it is only in desperation that Congress considers doing something about reproduction by passing an Emergency Bill. The world's natural resources have been used up because of the population explosion. Some of my young readers liked the book very much; others did not.

For a booktalk use facts from the opening chapter that show some of the shortages, the sordid conditions, and the way the police deal with riots. Also, a booktalker can point out what is now occurring in parts of Africa and in Brazil to show that the author has some basis for his ideas.

Young readers fascinated by *Unicorns in the Rain* by Barbara Cohen, in which the world appears to have become rotten and the members of a family believe they have found a way to escape, may also like *Make Room! Make Room!* In *No Room for Man*, the authors Ralph Clem, Martin Greenberg, and Joseph Olander take a serious look at the steady growth of the world's population and, through science-fiction short stories, forecast what the future may be unless something is done to slow the growth. These stories consider the impact of overpopulation: social consequences, food problems, effects on environment and resources. Possible solutions to great overcrowding are examined. Each section has a short introduction and a short bibliography in case the reader is interested in pursuing more factual information. A portion of Harrison's book is included. In *Time of the Fourth Horseman* by Chelsea Yarbro, another story of overpopulation, the government decides to use a controlled epidemic to decrease the number of people in the United States. However, the plan backfires, and horror is the result. A young person who is really interested in the population explosion might like to look at *You, Me, and a Few Billion More* by Jessma O. Blockwick, a paperback. It presents an unprejudiced look at the changing attitudes toward population growth in the world and at what is being done in various countries by international as well as local organizations.

Hart, Kitty

Return to Auschwitz. 1982. Atheneum.

Although Kitty Hart had spent eighteen months in Auschwitz, she begins her story with events after the war, when she and her mother were sent to relatives in England. She soon learned that the English did not want to hear about her wartime experiences. Feeling her story is important, she later returns to Auschwitz to review her experiences. In recounting them she harks back to the entry of the Germans into Bielsko, Poland, where she lived with her parents. They try and fail to escape to Russia, but Father Krasowski, one of her mother's pupils in English, obtains false identification papers for them. The family splits up: Kitty and her mother go as Poles to Germany to work in a factory, and her father works on a nearby farm. In a short time, Kitty and her mother are part of a group rounded up for questioning and accused of being Jews, and they spend time in various prisons before being sent to Auschwitz. There the hut for sleeping has tiers of bunks, each with room for one person though as many as five are at times crowded into each bunk. The first morning Kitty realizes that survival is determined by how quickly one learns the ways of the camp and its occupants. Kitty and her mother, who have served a kind of apprenticeship on the run, in the ghetto, and in prison, are somewhat hardened. Seeing that some girls have responsibilities and live better, Kitty is determined to be alert and learn quickly. Her mother is assigned to the hospital compound because the prisoners in charge are awed by the fact that she has been admitted to the camp instead of being sent to the death chambers. Kitty is fortunate that her mother, by working in the hospital, can nurse her through a bout with typhus and later with pneumonia. Eventually Kitty is assigned to sort contents of new arrivals' baggage and is able to smuggle towels, soap, and footwear into camp when she visits her mother. In 1944 she and her mother are transferred to work in a factory and later in an underground ammunition plant. Eventually they are liberated by the Americans. Her description of life in camp with poor food, exposure to the elements, lack of proper clothing, forced labor, cruel punishments, and overcrowding is horrifying.

The author had plenty of time between her liberation and her return to Auschwitz to do research on the camp. Thus she has included information that she did not have when she was imprisoned at the camp. This adds value to the book. She and her mother were political prisoners, which accounts for the few privileges they had, but they were also very astute and took advantage of every chance to better their circumstances. My young readers found the book fascinating and voted for its selection for annotation in preference to those titles used as follow-ups.

Two or three very brief descriptions of the family's attempts to elude the Germans in Poland might be used as a booktalk, pages 38–45. Several short episodes at Auschwitz could also be used, pages 70–76. Pages 96–101 tell of Kitty's punishment for trying to steal wood for a stove in their hut.

Isabella Leitner's *Fragments of Isabella* is appropriately titled as she includes only poignant bits and pieces of her experiences when she and her three sisters were at Auschwitz. In a very small book entitled *Childhood,* Jona Oberski describes his experiences as a young child in the Bergen-Belsen concentration camp. In *Gizelle, Save the Children* Gizelle Hersch describes how her Hungarian family is sent to the concentration camp in overcrowded cattle cars. Because she speaks German, she has to translate for Dr. Mengele, and she lies about the ages of her brother and three sisters. Her mother's last words are the title of the book. Gizelle cannot save Sander because boys have been sent to a different area, but she does save her sisters—at both Auschwitz and Dachau. In *Hanna and Walter: A Love Story,* the Kohners tell of falling in love before World War II. Though he is allowed to emigrate to the United States, she is not, and when the Germans round up the Jews in Holland, she is sent to Auschwitz. But near the end of the war, Walter comes to Germany and finds Hanna. In *Women at War* Kevin Sim tells suspenseful stories of "Five heroines who defied the Nazis and survived." Hiltgunt Zassenhaus wrote an account of her work during World War II in *Walls: Resisting the Third Reich—One Woman's Story,* which is annotated at length in the third edition of *Book Bait.* In *Invisible Walls* Ingeborg Hecht, daughter of a German mother and Jewish father, uses the Nuremberg Laws concerning Jews as an outline for her family's experiences in Germany from 1935 to the end of World War II.

Hawdon, Robin

A Rustle in the Grass.   1985.   Dodd, Mead.

This story about a colony of small ants opens with the death of its leader during the winter sleep. When the Council meets to decide what to do, several leaders who are not Council members attend, including Black Sting, commander of the soldier ants, and Noble, captain of the Royal Guard. When those attending are allowed to speak, old Five Legs, a worker, says that the workers should be represented on Council because they do all the work in the mound. At about the same time Dreamer, a soldier out on a scouting expedition, comes upon a small, excited ant from another mound. Huge red ants have attacked his home, and he is the lone survivor. Dreamer takes him to the Council, which sends one of Black Sting's lieutenants, Snake's Tongue, and two soldiers, Dreamer and Joker, to investigate. They find no living insects in the area around the plundered mound. Snake's Tongue decides they should search for the red ants' headquarters. Unfortunately, they are captured and imprisoned by the red ants, but they manage to escape. However, only Dreamer, after several close calls, gets home, where quite a few changes have been made. Workers are on Council, and soldiers help the workers in their duties. Shortly before the red ants reach the mound's area, a Giant Two-Legs is reported nearby. During the night he builds a fire in the ants' clearing. They have never seen fire and do not know what it is. When the giant leaves, he does not douse the fire. In the morning before the red ants' attack, Dreamer investigates the fire and talks with several of the oldest ants who have hidden nearby. Dreamer feels the heat, smells the smoke, and sees how the fire burns twigs and grass, but he doesn't understand it. The red ants arrive, and there is a desperate battle. When the last barriers to the mound are about to go, Dreamer hurries to the fire and, with the help of the old ants, cuts down a great clump of dead grass. He sets it afire and with it ignites other grass. The fire spreads quickly, incinerating not only the red ants and their leader but also most of the mound's ants. The next spring a small group of visiting ants comes to the mound and finds a blind, crippled Dreamer and many very young ants scurrying around him. When they ask what happened and offer assistance, he tells them the story.

Some of the best parts of this delightful tale are the stories that Still One tells. Each has a point that makes the listening ant think, and the listener is often Dreamer. He learns a great deal from the stories and from his adventures, and as a result he saves his colony even though most of the residents also die. The author is so skillful in developing his characters that the reader can't help becoming involved with them and their fate.

I have not had an opportunity to use this in a booktalk. It may be best to introduce the book to individual readers who you know will appreciate something unusual. They can then tell their friends about it. This will give you a chance to talk with them and get their reaction.

Richard Adams in *Watership Down* has done with rabbits what Hawdon did with ants, and each book can be suggested as a follow-up to the other. *The Quest for the Faradawn*° by Richard Ford tells of a group of animals and birds that adopt a baby boy left in their woods. Anyone who is especially fond of cats will enjoy *Tailchaser's Song* by Tod Williams. It describes the amazing adventures of Fritti Tailchaser, a young, apricot-orange male cat, and little Pouncequick, a brave and bouncing kitten, on a long trek to find Hushpad, the love of Fritti's life, which has mysteriously disappeared.

Hayden, Torey L.

One Child. 1980. Putnam.

At the beginning of the school year, the author, an educational psychologist, is assigned eight problem children. Their difficulties range from autism and retardation to schizophrenia and blindness. Three are not toilet trained. With the aid of a full-time assistant and of a junior high school girl for two hours an afternoon, Torey helps the children adjust to school, to one another, and to learning, until at last she actually looks forward to each new day. However, after Christmas six-year-old Sheila is brought into the room. She has tied a three-year-old boy to a tree and burned him so badly that he is in critical condition in a hospital. The court has sentenced her to a state hospital, but there is no opening. She is tiny, dirty, smelly, hostile, and silent. That first day, while aides are in charge of the class during the lunch period, the child kills most of the goldfish by poking their eyes out with a pencil, throwing the classroom into an uproar. But by the third day she begins to show some interest in the activities going on, and when Torey tests her, she is amazed at the results. Sheila can read at the fifth-grade level and is especially good in arithmetic, but she has a lot to learn about behavior. Some of those learning experiences are painful for everyone. Eventually Sheila improves, and when word comes that space at the state hospital is available, Torey knows it would be a dreadful mistake for the child to go there. She persuades her boyfriend, a lawyer, to go to court and petition the judge to allow Sheila to stay in school. At one point Sheila's uncle misuses her sexually, and she comes to school bleeding badly. When Torey discovers it, she rushes her to a hospital. Later Torey has to explain to the class what had happened. Earlier in the year the children had been warned against adults' touching them in wrong places, and so they had a little background for learning about Sheila's experience. Torey tells of various special events during the remainder of the year and of how difficult it is to tell Sheila that the next year she will go into a regular class and that Torey herself will be leaving the city to work on her Ph.D.

Librarians across the United States recommended this true story. All the junior high girls in my group who read the book endorsed it enthusiastically. Admitting that her methods of teaching special children are not always the recommended ones, the author states they work best for her, and, therefore, she uses them. She not only involves herself emotionally with the children but also her readers.

There are many episodes that can be used in a booktalk. Sheila destroys the aquarium, pages 35–44; cleaning Sheila up is a big job and cannot be done in one day, pages 71–79; Sheila's sense of revenge knows no limits, pages 95–104.

Murphy's Boy, also by Torey Hayden, concerns a boy of fifteen, silent and terrified, who seeks refuge under a table. Over the years that Torey works with him, he develops, by age eighteen, into a young man who wants to attend high school and make his own way in the world. More mature readers can be introduced to this book. While finishing her degree in elementary and special education, Mary McCracken worked with several problem children in a school. Like Torey Hayden, Mary has a special talent for working with disturbed children. One of her books is *City Kid.* In *If We Could Hear the Grass Grow* Eleanor Craig tells about twelve emotionally disturbed children and their bizarre experiences at a summer day camp she operates at her home. She is helped by three adult offspring and a young man who works at the clinic where she is employed.

Hennessy, Max

The Bright Blue Sky. 1983. Atheneum.

One Saturday in 1914 Dicken Quinney goes out to a field where he had heard that some idiot is going to fly and is more or less pushed into becoming a passenger. To his surprise he finds the flight a thrilling experience. When England enters the war in Europe, Dicken, who has a first-class certificate as a wireless operator, enlists. Shortly after he reaches France, he is transferred temporarily to the Flying Corps. Planes in those days are flimsy and slow, with a maximum altitude of 6,000 feet. Fortunately Dicken becomes friends with William Hatto, a pilot, who upon learning Dicken wants to join the RFC, helps him to get a transfer. Actually the war becomes a contest between English and German plane manufacturers, each designing new planes a little better than their opponents', but they never do invent a method of communication between the planes and the ground, and the flyers do not have parachutes. Hence, when a plane is shot down, the pilot and observer usually die. For some time Dicken is an observer who rides behind the pilot and operates the gun as part of his duties. Dicken seems to have no fear and before long has earned two or three decorations for bravery. Some of his experiences leave the reader breathless. Finally he applies and is accepted for pilot training. The British are losing so many pilots that they are desperate for replacements. A man from Dicken's home area, who knows the right people and has influence, has been transferred to Dicken's unit. When the pilots find out he has avoided danger spots, they nickname him "Parasol Percy." Eventually Dicken and Hatto are transferred to Italy where there are no accommodations for British flyers; for a while they are billeted with families, and Dicken falls in love with the older daughter of the family with whom he stays but marriage is not allowed. Flying against the Austrians is easier than against the Germans, and Dicken shoots down many more planes and is awarded another medal. He has escaped serious injury up to this time, but he is badly wounded shortly before the war ends, when he is again flying in France.

There is a lot of action in the story, and the characters are appealing. The author writes well. Young readers, both boys and girls, are fascinated by those primitive machines and the men who dared fly them.

Dicken's first ride in an airplane has some humor in it and could be used in a booktalk, pages 3–9. His rescue of Hatto from an overturned plane about to explode is short and also has a touch of humor, pages 39–41.

The Challenging Heights continues Dicken's experiences after the war as the RAF struggles for existence. He is sent to Iraq, where rival tribes are fighting; to China where the government, and Communists, and Chiang Kai-shek are at war; and to India where tribes are battling. This sequel needs a reader who is interested in the history of areas in the news today. *Once More the Hawks* tells of World War II. B-17 combat crews were required to take part in twenty-five missions over Europe before they could be assigned to duty back in the United States. In *Combat Crew* John Comer gives a day-by-day account of his agonizing experiences as a Flight engineer–gunner while he accumulates the necessary missions and watches plane after plane go down in flames.

Herbert, Marie

Winter of the White Seal.   1982.   Morrow.

Though he has a fine education and prospects for the future, Jonathan Horn, son of a well-to-do merchant in England, longs for adventure. One night in 1818 he goes down to the docks and signs on the *Moonraker*, a sealer, the worst kind of ship known to man. They sail to South Georgia near Antarctica. All the safe harbors near the sealing beaches have been taken, but finally they find an undiscovered area where there are many elephant and fur seals. Then the slaughter begins. Sometime later the ship fires a recall; ominous black clouds are building rapidly, and the men are in a frenzy to get aboard because there is more room to maneuver in the open sea. Jonathan has come upon a beautiful white seal and its pup and sees the mate making for the mother seal, but he is unable to stop him. Jonathan is knocked out, and it is evening before he regains consciousness. That night he hears a baby seal crying. It sounds different from the others, and he follows the cry. The little creature has fallen into a cleft in the rocks and cannot get out. Jonathan retrieves it and sees that it is white. The mother has disappeared. Though hungry, the baby does not care for the warm seal stew his rescuer is eating. At daylight Jonathan begins to look for a foster mother, but none will accept the orphan. At length he sees a seal give birth to a stillborn. He snatches it up and smears the white seal with the afterbirth. This mother allows the baby to nurse. When the ship does not return, Jonathan knows he will have to make a permanent shelter, kill enough seals to provide food for the winter, and make some warm clothing for himself. He knows the seals and penguins will leave before winter begins. When the pup's adopted mother does not return from a feeding expedition, Jonathan has the responsibility of the baby again. By this time the pup will eat some solid food. Jonathan names it Scruff, and it begins to follow him about as he works. When winter begins, he is quite proud of his preparations, but, alas, many things go wrong. He probably would have given up and died in his sleep had it not been for Scruff. Jonathan cuts his rations and grows thin and weak; by this time Scruff is big enough to swim and find his own food. One time the pup saves Jonathan's life when he becomes lost in a blizzard. In the spring the seals come back, and he realizes that if he is rescued he cannot take Scruff with him. Embarking on a long trek, he leaves Scruff behind, and when he returns at the beginning of the second winter, the young seal is gone. During the second summer of his isolation Jonathan is rescued.

The description of the killing of the seals early in the story turns off some readers, but from then on there is plenty of interest, particularly when Scruff comes into the story. The author and her husband lived for two years with the Eskimos of northwest Greenland, and thus she had firsthand knowledge of living in Arctic conditions. She spent five years in researching and writing, and her book shows the care she took. The story is lively, informative, and often entertaining. Young adult librarians heartily recommend this book.

After telling how Jonathan acquired Scruff as a companion, the booktalker could describe how the baby became Jonathan's sleeping companion, pages 117–19. On the occasion when Jonathan discovers usable flotsam on the neighboring beach, he forgets to watch the clouds and is caught in a terrible storm. There are several incidents within this experience on pages 141–48, one or two of which could be used in a booktalk. Some of the events in the chapter entitled "The Big Storm," pages 160–67, could also be used.

The White Shaman by Clive Nicol is an unusually well-written story of an eighteen-year-old boy who does the dirty work at a university professor's research camp in northern Canada one summer. Because the boy has an affinity for the area, its wildlife, and the Inuit hunters, he loves what he has to do. There is an unexpected and sad ending. In *Cry of the Seals* Jeremy Lucas tells of a research team studying birthrates and making comparisons of growth in harp and hooded seals on the ice pack off Newfoundland. Because the team has won the trust of the seals, the men try to defend the animals when the sealers come to slaughter the baby seals. The story ends in tragedy.

Herring, Robert

Hub. 1981. Viking.

Hub, the young son of a respected family in an Arkansas city, is intrigued by some of the tales his friend Hitesy tells. That lad comes from a broken home, has very little supervision, and knows about the seamy side of life. One night he persuades Hub to join him after his parents are asleep and go window peeping at a prostitute's shack. It is not sex they witness but violence. Lute Freeman, a retarded adult, is drunk when he breaks down the door of the woman's shanty. As Lute is trying to force himself upon her, the woman sees one of the boys at the window and tries to ask for help. Lute catches on and throws her aside as he takes off after the boys. Hub and Hitesy escape, and Lute goes back to the shack to find the woman dead. Walking back to the city Lute is picked up by the man who drives the heating oil truck. Lute murders him and drives the truck into the river instead of making a getaway. He hides nearby on a large piece of land, which at high water is an island in the Mississippi River. On one end of that island lives an old man whom Hub had met when he was exploring, and the two had become friends. Hub calls him Uncle Ethel and loves to visit him because the old man's stories and knowledge of nature fascinate him. The day after their nighttime adventure, Hub takes Hitesy to meet him. They tell the old man about the remains of a small fire they found at the end of the island. That night Uncle Ethel thinks he hears someone in his garden. Thereafter he carries his gun wherever he goes. The sheriff's deputy comes by and tells him he is looking for Lute. Uncle Ethel sets up three ingenious traps that could kill or badly injure Lute. One day Lute comes close and asks for food. He has an iron pipe in his hand, and when he tries to get closer, the old man fires, hitting him in the leg, but Lute gets away. Shortly the boys bring a tent out to the island and decide to camp close to the cabin. The old man sits at a window on guard most of the night. Early the next morning Hub goes exploring. When Uncle Ethel learns that, he quickly begins to track him, knowing Lute might catch him. The boy is trapped, but fate intervenes, and Hub gets away while Lute suffers more injury. Later Lute falls into the river and is swept away.

The story is very well told, and the characters are well drawn. The old man's skill in instilling courage in the boys, their obedience to his instructions, and their faith in and respect for him are very satisfying for the reader. A description of schoolboys tormenting Lute and the nasty thoughts of the oil-truck man who has to deliver oil after normal working hours to an old woman are regrettable scenes but un.doubtedly true to life. The best use of this book is for a teacher or parent to read it aloud and follow each event with discussion.

Several episodes are possibilities for booktalks. An explanation of why Uncle Ethel lives alone on the island, pages 64–78; Uncle Ethel finds his dead dog and footprints and sets three traps, pages 102–8; or Hub and Hitesy visit Uncle Ethel and Hub catches a glimpse of a figure escaping from the corner of the cabin, pages 111–13.

Also suggest *I Am One of You Forever* by Fred Chappell. He tells of ten-year-old Jess's escapades with his best friend, an eighteen-year-old orphan who works on the farm and shares his room, and Joe Robert, his dad, who has never really grown up and is always thinking up some outlandish trick to play on someone.

Hersey, John

Hiroshima.   1948.   Knopf.

John Hersey has recreated the nuclear destruction of the Japanese city of Hiroshima by tracing the lives of six people who lived through the awful day in August 1945. When the atomic bomb explodes, Toshiko Sasaki has just sat down in her office at the East Asia Tin Works. Dr. Masakazu Fujii is reading the Osaka *Asahi* on the porch of his private hospital. Father Wilhelm Kleinsorge, a German priest of the Society of Jesus, is reading a Jesuit magazine on the top floor of his mission house. Mrs. Hatsuyo Nakamura stands by her kitchen window watching her neighbor tear down his house to make room for an air-raid defense fire lane. Dr. Terufumi Sasaki, a member of the surgical staff of the Red Cross Hospital, is walking along the hospital corridor with a blood specimen in his hand. The Reverend Kiyoshi Tanimoto, pastor of the Methodist church, has stopped at the door of a suburban house to unload a handcart full of things he is evacuating from the city. One hundred thousand people are killed by the atomic bomb, and these six are among those who survive. Why have they lived when so many others have died? In clear, reportorial style, Hersey recounts the events of August 6 and the days following as they are recalled by these six. Small items of chance—being inside instead of outdoors, taking one streetcar instead of another, sitting beside bookcases—contributed to their survival. There is no word of reproach, no attempt to understand the horror and the calamity. The author has drawn no explicit moral. The facts speak dramatically and tragically for themselves.

Teenagers who are fascinated by the event at Hiroshima find this book a moving experience. The unvarnished, ugly facts of the suffering caused by the atomic bomb explosion are not pleasant reading, but young adults interested in the welfare of the world's people surely need to know the inhumanness of atomic warfare as portrayed in this slim volume.

Mentioning the name Hiroshima may be the only introduction that the book needs, for the city and what happened there are familiar to most. For some groups the first part of the foregoing annotation could be used for a brief introduction.

No High Ground by Fletcher Knebel gives a similar account of several people who were in Hiroshima at the time, but it also includes a history of the atomic bomb, an account of the decision to drop it, and the story of the plane that flew the bomb to Japan. In *Enola Gay* Gordon Thomas gives a very detailed account of the training of the 509th Composite Group, which dropped the first atomic bomb. The activities of the squadron on and off the base alternate with descriptions of some of the problems encountered by scientists working on the bomb, decisions made by President Truman and the U.S. military leaders, and first-hand stories of Japanese military, civilian, and government personnel at Hiroshima and Tokyo. If you don't have these, try a more recently published book—*Day One: Before Hiroshima and After* by Peter Wyden. He gives a detailed account of the construction of the atomic and nuclear bombs and of the famous scientists who worked on them. These men had no conception of the vast destructiveness of the bombs. It is interesting to note that some scientists urged that an international conference be organized to keep control of nuclear weapons and their use, but these men were ignored. He also tells of individuals who survived and of what they saw, experienced, and did.

Higgins, Jack

Day of Judgment. 1979. Holt.

Jack Higgins has built his story around an actual historical event. The Communists in East Germany are determined to make President Kennedy's visit to West Germany in the spring of 1963 worthless as a diplomatic gesture. To do that they need to capture Father Sean Conlin, head of the League of the Resurrection, a Christian underground movement that smuggles people out of East Germany. If they can get Father Conlin to admit—at a public trial—his involvement with the CIA and the espionage activities against East Germany, the testimony will have a damaging effect on Kennedy's visit to Berlin. They bribe Margaret Campbell, by promising her she will be permitted to see her terminally ill father, to carry a message to Conlin that will bring him secretly into East Germany. Too late, she learns that she has been deceived, and in attempting to escape, she loses her footing and rolls down the bank of the flooded Elbe River. When she disappears in the middle of the river, the guards think she has drowned. She is found draped over a fallen tree in the river by a brother of the Franciscan Order of Jesus and Mary. When the Franciscans hear her story, they immediately go into action. Father Conlin is a prisoner at the nearby Schloss Newstadt. The brothers supply the village with milk, and when Brother Konrad takes milk to the inn, he talks with the caretaker of the castle and learns there are twenty guards, a sergeant, and a captain at the castle. He agrees to supply them with milk. The League of the Resurrection smuggles Konrad into West Germany. He goes to Major Vaughn, also involved in smuggling at the Berlin Wall, and sets the plan of rescue in motion Father Conlin's experiences in the castle and the rescue effort alternate. The plan involves digging a tunnel from the Home Farm to meet the sewer that has never been completed at the castle, bribing the caretaker at the castle, bribing the guards at a little-used crossing of the Berlin Wall, getting a former German pilot to fly a small plane into a deserted airfield not far from the village, and getting everyone participating in the rescue safely out of East Berlin. Although the time to accomplish all this is limited, the plan works, and the East German plan is foiled.

A *dramatis personae* is really needed at the beginning of the book so that the reader can easily identify the many characters who are rapidly introduced as the story starts. The tension is high, action is probably implausible, and interest is easily maintained. There is not a great deal of character development, but in this type of high adventure, it is unimportant.

In a booktalk introduce Father Conlin and his rescue work. The priest had been imprisoned during World War II and had survived the hell of Dachau and Sasksenhausen. He wants to do things his own way, and he totally disregards any kind of authority, including the Vatican. The Pope has even censured him at one time. He has been recommended for the Nobel Peace Prize but had to turn it down because the Church did not approve. Pages 17–19 tell how he is captured by the East Germans, and pages 44–45 describe the cell in which he is imprisoned at the castle. An indication that a rescue plan will be attempted should spur readers to read the book.

As a follow-up, suggest *Cloak of Darkness* by Helen MacInnes. It is a complicated story having to do with an American, an Englishman, and a Frenchman, all ex–NATO intelligence men, who have set up a new organization called Interintel that works mostly against organized terrorists. The story follows one of the cases on which they are working, which involves smuggling, murder, and violence. MacInnes also wrote *The*

Hidden Target, a story about international terrorists who expect to cause so much despair and confusion that they can take over the world. A mild love story is included. *Judgment in St. Peter's* by Aaron Rotsstein takes place during World War II. Several families have been sadly affected by the ruthless actions of Iorga, a Nazi Iron Guardist in Bucharest and Rome. When a young Italian priest is arrested in Uruguay in 1977, his picture in newspapers draws the attention of several persons in the United States, Italy, and Spain. The priest resembles Iorga closely. Wanting to avenge Iorga's acts, they come to Italy when the priest is released and sent home to Rome. They hope to locate Iorga and get revenge. An experienced reader of this genre can tackle the quite long and complicated *The Red Fox* by Anthony Hyde. It tells of a young journalist seeking to solve a mystery half a century old. Pursued by a Soviet agent, he flies to Europe and Russia and back to the United States as bits of information fall into place.

Hofvendahl, Russ

Hard on the Wind.   1983.   Morrow.

In April 1937 Russ and his friend Herb cut their afternoon high school classes and wander down the Embarcadero in San Francisco. Both want very much to go to sea, but to ship out on an American vessel, one has to belong to the union. Later, as they walk down Clay Street, they see men in front of the Union Fish Company. As they reach the group, they hear a voice say, "Ok, last berth. We need a messman." Herb speaks up quickly, saying he'll take that job. Neither of them knows where the ship is going. Herb's father will not let him go, and Russ goes down to the office early the next morning to take Herb's place. When Russ gets his papers at the U.S. Maritime Commission Offices, he changes his date of birth so it will be two years earlier. Russ's father is dead and his mother hospitalized with tuberculosis; he lives with an uncle. When he reaches the ship, he discovers it is a sailing vessel bound for the Bering Sea to fish for cod. He soon learns there are two groups of men aboard: the fishermen and the dress gang who gut and salt the cod. The next morning Russ is assigned to the third watch led by the third mate. Although he has been signed on as messman, he doesn't get the job. Instead he becomes an idler on the dress gang. *Idler* is a sarcastic word for one of the hardest jobs on deck when the men are fishing. During his watch, Russ is told to take the wheel. Steering the ship is difficult at first, but the third mate is a good teacher. Russ's next learning experience is setting some sails, and Chris Olsen, an experienced man, works with him. Russ is full of questions, and the men are invariably decent about answering, even when the question seems silly to them. Russ is a hard worker and always willing to help someone out or take on an extra job. He likes to listen to the men telling stories of their lives at sea. The U.S. Coast Guard patrols the area, bringing them mail and taking off a sick or injured man. The crew has great respect for the sailors on the Coast Guard vessel. When the ship finally has its load of fish, it is unable to get through Unimak Pass and out into the Pacific because the wind dies or changes direction. Finally the little Coast Guard vessel has to take them in tow.

There are many exciting moments in this true sea story. The author has made a number of the people come alive. Because Russ thinks sailors should be experienced sexually, he spends two dollars in a red-light district and a much longer time worrying about venereal disease. Most of the men are Scandinavians, and the author uses broken English when they speak. There is some profanity, as might be expected, but it is not particularly offensive.

Russ's first turn at the wheel would make a good booktalk because not only is he learning something new but also a still partly drunk crew member takes the wheel away from him and turns the ship back toward San Francisco, pages 27–31. Another episode is his first climb at night to help get the main tops'l down with a hard wind blowing. He almost doesn't make it as he goes up on the wrong side of the sails, pages 54–58. A fire on board is another possibility, pages 68–73.

A different type of story about a boy at sea in a very small sailing vessel is *Dove*. Here Robin Lee Graham tells of his experiences sailing alone around the world, stopping as long as he likes so as to satisfy his desire to get to know people native to various areas. He also meets the girl he marries—a Californian working her way around the world. See Wortman's *Almost Too Late* for other books on near disasters at sea.

Johanson, Donald, and *Edey, Matiland A.*

Lucy: The Beginning of Humankind. 1981. Simon & Schuster.

The authors give a brief history of discoveries of the bones of early humans in Germany, France, Java, and China in the latter half of the nineteenth century. There were rivalries among early scientists and disagreements about the ages of the fossils found. Johanson becomes interested in anthropology in high school and chooses to attend the University of Chicago because the head of the anthropology program is Clark Howell, who has wide experience as a field worker in Spain and Ethiopia. The authors describe the work of Louis Leakey, who was born in Kenya and made important discoveries in Tanzania and Ethiopia when others scoffed at the possibility of finding ancient man in that area. In 1970 Johanson, then a postgraduate, meets Howell in Nairobi and South Africa, where he has a chance to handle some of Leakey's famous discoveries. He has his first field experience in Omo in Ethiopia, where other scientists are also working. In 1971, he returns to Omo, where he meets Maurice Taieb, a French geologist interested in working in the Afar Triangle in Ethiopia. Taieb offers Johanson a chance to work there in 1972. He has not finished his dissertation and does not yet have his Ph.D. when he is offered a position at Case Western Reserve University in Cleveland teaching anthropology. He agrees to accept if they will give him $1,000 so that he can join Taieb. The two men investigate the Afar area and decide it is worth organizing a formal expedition. Johanson finds the knee joint of a hominid, a very valuable fossil. That year he finishes the work for his Ph.D. before he leaves for Afar. In 1974 he finds Lucy, which is the most complete, oldest, and best-preserved specimen found to this time. Johanson and Taieb spend two more years in that area but are not permitted to return because of political upheaval in Ethiopia. The American team has accumulated many fossils that need analyzing. The authors explain how this is done, what they discover about their fossils, and how they establish criteria for the different ages of their discoveries. As a matter of fact, they have to design a new family tree for man. Richard Leakey and his mother carried on Louis Leakey's work after he died and have made important discoveries also. They do not agree with Johanson and his team's analysis of fossils.

The authors of *Lucy* write well, the account moves nicely, and it does not get too technical. Some readers may bog down in the last two chapters, which go into the research done or still to be done on the fossils.

The discovery of Lucy, pages 14–24, makes very interesting booktalks. Another important discovery may be found on pages 213–17.

The *National Geographic* for November 1985, is a good introduction to factual information about prehistoric discoveries. Lucy is, of course, the star. In *One Life* Richard E. Leakey, son of the famous Louis Leakey, tells of growing up in Kenya as an African. At first he is not much interested in his father's search for prehistoric remains. Before he finishes secondary school, he begins to capture animals for a photographer for British television, and this leads to organizing African safaris and hunting expeditions, both of which are exciting. Eventually he begins to explore as his father did and makes a career in that field and as a museum director. *Ascent to Civilization: The Archaeology of Early Man* by John Gowlett begins with the first signs of man found in the Rift Valley region and—with text, drawings, maps, and photographs—shows how man developed. Johanson and the Leakeys are mentioned as well as many other scientists who have worked through the years to uncover man's development. In *The Search for the Past* L. B. Halstead begins with rocks to trace the development of the earth. Then he tells about fossils and how we can trace the evolution of plants and animals. Abundantly illustrated in color, the book is good for browsing as well as for serious reading. Please refer to the entry for Jean Auel on page 1 for other books on the subject of early man.

Johnson, Eric W.

Love and Sex in Plain Language.   1985.   Harper.

Believing that almost everyone, no matter what their age, is interested in sex, Johnson first wrote this book in 1965. Parents, counselors, teachers, and teenagers have found it so useful that the book has been revised three times. The author begins by briefly listing eight values that teenagers should consider in making decisions about sex. He discusses the physical structure of female and male sex organs with appropriate diagrams. He explains sexual intercourse briefly and tells how fertilization takes place in the female's body. Then he outlines the development of a fetus and describes how a baby is born. The author maintains that homosexuality exists in some people just as heterosexuality does in others—that it is not a matter of choice. He discusses masturbation, molestation, incest, rape, and the special problems of teenage pregnancy. He considers family planning important in order to control world population; thus, methods of birth control are given attention. There is a chapter on sexually transmitted diseases, and Johnson warns about the sexual influence of popular songs, movies, TV, and advertising. A complete glossary gives pronunciations and definitions as well as page numbers for more information. A mastery test concludes the book so that persons may test themselves on their knowledge of the subject.

The book is straightforward and well done and gives information that is adequate for many teenagers.

Librarians will probably not use this type of book for a book-talk, but they should know the contents of sex-education guides in their collection so that they can recommend to students those best suited to their particular needs.

In *What's Happening to My Body? Book for Boys* and *What's Happening to My Body? A Growing Up Guide for Girls and Their Mothers,* Lynda Madaras chattily discusses puberty and tries to allay any fears that boys and girls might have about what is or is not happening to their bodies. She teaches sex education in elementary and high school and draws on experiences there in presenting her information. She is less restrained in her discussion than Johnson, and some communities may prefer Johnson to Madaras.

Jones, Douglas C.

Elkhorn Tavern.   1980.   Holt.

The family of Martin Hasford lives on a farm in western Arkansas, and when Martin joins the Confederate Army, he leaves his wife, Ora, fifteen-year-old son, Roman, and seventeen-year-old daughter, Calpurnia, to take care of it. All are very capable, but the marauding jayhawkers and bushwackers

84

could make their lives difficult. Some of the neighbors favor the South, others the North. But all are too busy to make a big thing out of their differences, except for Spider Epp. By joining one of the guerrilla bands, Spider hopes to get even with those who had looked down on him. But when the Union cavalry patrols begin coming down Wire Road through the area, the raiders stay away. In March, 1862, the Southern Army begins the trek north toward Elkhorn Tavern, where the Union troops are fortifying the bluffs along Little Sugar Creek, not far from the Hasford farm. The two armies eventually take their positions, and the Southerners build large bonfires at night in their camp. In the morning the Union soldiers see that the Confederate camp is deserted. The Southerners have quietly marched north and come in behind the Union forces. The author describes the battle, which rages for several days. The Confederates, finally short of ammunition, have to withdraw, taking many of their wounded with them. A member of the Cherokee brigade, who has had enough, deserts, and late the next day comes across a wounded Union officer in the woods. It is night before he brings the man to the Hasford farm. Taking the man in, Ora discovers that blood poisoning has set in and the man is delirious. She sends Roman for an old neighbor who has a little knowledge of caring for wounds. Jones tells in some detail how they amputate part of the man's lower arm. The patient survives but takes a long time to recuperate. Meanwhile he falls in love with Calpurnia. There is an impressive scene in which Ora interviews the young man about his intentions concerning her daughter. All ends well.

Douglas Jones has presented a good array of strong characters, and he has provided enough suspense with raids, battles, the wounded man, and budding romance to hold the reader's interest.

The guerrilla raid in the area and at the Hasford farm should be sufficient to introduce main characters and establish the time of the story and some of the anxiety experienced by the settlers, pages 3–25.

Also suggest *The Barefoot Brigade*, a powerful novel in which Jones gives a picture of the Civil War quite different from the one above. The principal character is seventeen-year-old Noah Fawley, sentenced to join the Confederate Army for the teenage prank of stealing a pig. He and his companions, farmers from Arkansas, take part in the major battles of the war. *Elkhorn Tavern* has a sequel but please bear in mind before recommending it to many junior high readers that it includes very rough language, much drinking, questionable business practices, and drugs. This sequel, *Roman*, is not recommended for junior high readers. See Stephen Crane on page 31 for other books on the Civil War.

Jones, Douglas C.

Season of Yellow Leaf. 1983. Holt.

In 1838 a band of Comanches attacks a small settlement of Welsh immigrants about a hundred miles from San Antonio, Texas, and carries off Morfydd Annow Parry, aged ten, and Dafydd, four. Stripped of their clothing, the captives are tied to captured horses. That night the leader of the Indians gives Morfydd water, and the next day he gives her clothing because she is badly sunburned. That afternoon half the group splits off, taking Dafydd with them. At night the leader tells Morfydd his name is Sanchess and gives her water and meat. Henceforth the warriors call the girl Chosen. When they reach their encampment, Sanchess tells his wife, Sunshade, to make some clothing for Chosen and to teach her to help with the work. On the way to winter quarters, they kill buffalo, whose meat is dried for storage. As time passes, Chosen becomes a good rider and often helps the boys with the pony herding. Before long an Indian named Wolfe's Road shows his interest in her by playing his cedar flute outside Sanchess's lodge. The time comes when the tribe discovers that white men kill buffalo for their hides and leave the meat to rot, something the Indians never do. That year there are fewer buffalo for their winter food. One day Come Behind, wife of Sanchess's father, Iron Shirt, walks out of camp to pick some spring flowers. She is not back by nightfall, and Sanchess is unable to find her. The next day one of the elders sees vultures wheeling low over the horizon. Sanchess and the young men ride out and find her, naked, raped, scalped, and her belly cut open. The unborn child she had been carrying would have been a daughter. Sanchess and four warriors who followed the trail overtake and kill the murderers. After this event Sanchess gives Chosen to Iron Shirt as a daughter to replace the baby who has been lost. Eventually she does become the wife of Wolfe's Road and they have a son, whom they name Kwahadi. Near the end of the story white soldiers attack the camp, killing many of the people. Chosen's blue eyes give her away, and she is taken to a white settlement. Sunshade with Kwahadi escapes the massacre and makes her way to Palo Duro, where the tribe often wintered. Sunshade tells the boy that his mother had been white, and he promises that he will find her some day and bring her back.

Douglas Jones writes very well and draws the reader into the story as a close observer. His characters are very real people. He has dedicated the book to the maternal grandmother of his good friend, Fred Brown, who is a Comanche and his valued consultant and critic.

The telling of the raid on the Welsh settlement, Morfydd's being kidnapped, and her first days with the Comanches may be enough to interest listeners in reading the book. Or on pages 62–69, Morfydd's plan to escape is foiled twice, and she decides she is better off staying with the Indians. The death of Come Behind may be found on pages 146–56 if the book talker prefers this episode.

The sequel, *Gone the Dreams and Dancing*, is a powerful story, brilliantly told, of Kwahadi, son of Chosen and Wolfe's Road. With the occasional aid of Liverpool Morgan, a white man the Comanches trust, Kwahadi is able to help his people adjust to life on a reservation and also to improve their lot. Allan W. Eckert, in *Johnny Logan, Shawnee Spy*, tells of Spemica Lawha, who is captured by Gen. Benjamin Logan in 1786. Because he has proven himself a brave twelve-year-old and speaks some English, he becomes a member of Logan's family and is named Johnny. In less than five months, there is a prisoner exchange and the boy is returned to his tribe. He admires so much what he has learned about white education and culture that he can never again fight against the whites, even though this leads to untold pain for his family and for himself. In *A Woman of the People* by Benjamin Capps two small white girls are carried off by a band of Comanches. The older, Helen, is determined to escape and take her sister with her, but she never has an opportunity until after her marriage to Burning Hand. Then, given a choice, she stays with the Indians. This fine story has been out of print but has recently been brought out by the University of New Mexico Press. The People were divided into five bands who meet annually for the Sun Dance, and *The Elk-dog Heritage* by Don Coldsmith is concerned mainly with a southern band that has a group of rebellious young warriors who are expelled by the People at a Sun Dance meeting. This leaves the southern band in very precarious circumstances. Most of the story focuses on attacks by an enemy tribe called the Head Splitters and of the way in which this courageous southern band faces probable elimination. Also suggest *Blue Savage* by Earl Murray. It tells of a white boy adopted by an Indian family. He resents being traded after several years to the white men for horses and is unhappy away from the Indians. As an adult, he rejoins the tribe and makes a place for himself. In a beautifully told story, *Song of the Meadowlark*, John A. Sanford takes the reader on the trail the Nez Perce Indians followed as they fled from American soldiers in an effort to reach safety in Canada. The main character, Teeto Hoonod, describes the hardship, battles, and escapes, his love for his young wife and his older brother, and tragedy and defeat.

Kennedy, John F.

Profiles in Courage.   1961.   Harper.

Right or wrong, all the men the author chose as examples of courage were convinced that their course of action was the best for the United States. Usually they were vilified for their decisions; sometimes vindication came during their lifetime. Each chose to sacrifice his political career, if necessary, rather than vote against his principles. These men were: John Quincy Adams, who believed that private interest must not be put in opposition to the public good; Daniel Webster, who voted in favor of the Compromise of 1850 in order to preserve the Union and thereby defied the people of his state; Thomas Hart Benton and Sam Houston, both of whom put the preservation of the Union before their constituents' opinions on slavery; Edmund G. Ross, whose vote in 1868 saved President Andrew Johnson from being impeached; Lucius Lamar, a Southerner, who dared to stand with the North after the Civil War when he thought the bill before Congress was for the good of the whole country, even though it did not benefit his state at the time;

George W. Norris, who deserted his party's stand when he thought it was wrong; and Robert A. Taft, who spoke out against the death sentences given at the Nuremberg trials, although most Americans felt them to be just. A senator experiences tremendous pressures that influence the stand he takes on any issue. He must consider his party's position, the desires of his constituents, conflicting ideas of special-interest groups, the opinions of his colleagues, and his own pride in office. Believing that as a nation we had forgotten courageous acts of the past, Mr. Kennedy wrote this book as a reminder. He maintains, "A nation which has forgotten the quality of courage which in the past has been brought to public life is not likely to insist upon or regard that quality in its chosen leaders today. . . . "

Stories of courageous statesmen appeal to the idealism of young people, especially in view of the corruption evident in all levels of government in recent years.

Any of the chapters could be used for a booktalk.

Recommend this book to readers who responded favorably to A Special Kind of Courage by Geraldo Rivera. He tells of eleven children and teenagers who he thought were especially courageous because of the ways they responded to difficult or dangerous situations. Although Many a Voyage by Loula Erdman is a good family story, it is also a fictionalized account of the life of Edmund Ross, whose love for his country and for justice made him risk his life many times.

Knowles, Anne

Matthew Ratton. 1981. St. Martin's.

Although Matthew Ratton had grown up on a farm, he does not intend to remain there. When his brother was killed in an accident, their father demanded that Matthew leave school and take David's place. Resentfully, Matthew accepted his fate. One hot summer the hay barn caught fire and the adjacent buildings also burned. Three times his well-trained dog, Trig, went into the barn to drive the cows out. On Trig's last trip, a burning beam fell, trapping her, and Matthew was badly burned trying to rescue her. As the story opens, Matthew is twenty-nine and almost a recluse because of the scar tissue on his face. John and Peggy Davey, the closest neighbors, have always been friendly and helpful, and the postman leaves Matthew's mail in their box. One day when collecting his mail, Matthew sees a tiny puppy lying outside the washhouse. Thinking this one of the litter too little and weak to survive, John has placed it there, intending to bury it later. When Matthew picks it up, he can feel its tiny heart still beating. As he has never replaced Trig, he decides to try to save the pup. He names her Jet because of her color and does save her. Jet is as carefully trained as Trig had been. In England bridle paths cut across farms, and Matthew is quite surly to a young woman who rides across his land several times, thinking she is probably a wealthy socialite visiting in the area. Matthew has no phone, and one day when a heifer is having difficulty calving, he stops the woman as she rides by and asks her to phone the veterinarian for him. After looking at the heifer, Mary West scrubs, does what needs to be done, and a fine calf is born. Matthew is reluctantly grateful. Later he learns that she is a medical nurse who has inherited a piece of land adjoining his. One night Matthew for the first time helps John celebrate his birthday at the pub. Later the pub owner encourages Matthew to enter Jet in a small local entertainment in which a dog demonstrates its herding ability with a small band of sheep. Matthew agrees, and Jet does very well. At home that evening Matthew becomes ill and in the morning is unable to milk his cows. John hears them bellowing and comes to investigate. Peggy nurses Matthew, and Mary takes turns with her. During his convalescence, Matthew and Mary decide they are in love and will marry later. Near the end of the story Matthew and Jet enter a serious competition for sheep dogs, and Jet wins.

Because its title is not attractive, the book will have to be introduced by the librarian. A good many junior high readers do not want to read dog stories, but this should be recommended to the few who enjoy them. Action is plentiful and the characters are true to life. There are a few words and customs that may be a bit strange to American young people, but they are not a deterrent.

Several incidents can be used for booktalks. Tell about Matthew's finding the puppy and how it displayed its instinct for herding when it was only eight weeks old, pages 20–22, 30–31. One day Matthew goes to town to buy some lumber and sees the savage dog kept at the yard to protect it from thieves. When the lumberyard goes out of business, the foreman is to dispose of the dog. However, it escapes and later attacks Matthew and Jet, pages 55, 60–63, 94–98. Jet does well at her first experience herding in public, pages 125–28.

Another story in which a dog takes part in and wins herding trials is *Nops's Trials* by Donald McCaig. This is a much longer book and is a family story in which various problems are worked out. A jealous dog owner pays someone to kidnap Nop, and the dog has great difficulties before his owner retrieves him. In *Laska,* a true story by Ronald Rood, a dog, three-quarters Siberian husky and one-quarter wolf, is the central character in a book that is often entertaining and certainly informative. In *The Lurcher* by Frank Walker, the dog is part greyhound and part collie. It had belonged to a gypsy and had protected his caravan. When the gypsy dies, the lurcher is loose without supervision, and sheep farmers fear for their flocks. While the search is on to kill the animal, several others are hunting it to capture and save it. *Shawno* is a sensitively written book in which George Dennison describes the large, handsome, golden-haired dog that lives with him in New York and in the country. He tells of the dog's devotion to the family, his favorite people, and his untimely end.

Knowles, John

Peace Breaks Out.   1981.   Holt.

In 1945 Pete Hallam, who had been a soldier in World War II, wounded in Italy, captured, and imprisoned, comes back to Devon School where he had taught before the war. He is an instructor in American history and a member of the physical education staff. In his very first class he discovers the animosity between Wexford, editor of the school newspaper, and Eric Hochschwender, who looks down on Americans as very poor quality. Neither boy is popular at school. Wexford is underhanded, finding various ways to get out of the physical education requirements and looking for news items that will stir up trouble. Although he is not eighteen, he looks older and so is able to buy liquor. Pete is concerned about the continued ill will between the boys in class and calls them in for a talk, but he actually settles nothing. Suddenly Wexford gets an inspiration to raise money for a stained-glass window in the chapel to honor former Devon students killed in the war. The idea is accepted, money comes in, and before long the window is installed. Pete takes a few of the boys who like to ski on two weekend excursions. The second time they go to the high mountains, and one of the football players dares to ski down from a difficult place. He falls, is injured, and is brought back to the infirmary at school. The next day the students and faculty discover that the new window has been knocked out and shattered. Wexford insinuates that Eric might well have done it. One day Eric rows his scull up the Devon River, and four boys in two canoes overtake him, dump him from his scull, and make him swim to shore. Then they haul him back into the water and dunk him. They tell him they will continue to do this until he confesses to breaking the window. After a few times Eric faints. Scared, the boys take him to the school infirmary. The experience has been too much for Eric, who has a rheumatic heart, and he dies. When the boys are questioned, they say that he collapsed in his scull and they brought him back to campus. Later the reader is led to believe it probably was Wexford who destroyed the window. Pete suspects him and wonders what kind of man he will become with this kind of start as a teenager.

The author's portrayal of the boys is not particularly appealing, but it is probably true to life. The war ended before their chance came to be heroes, and obviously they find other ways to draw attention to themselves. The book was not universally approved by my group, but it gave them something about which to think.

Perhaps the best way to introduce the main juvenile characters is to tell about Pete's first history class and the animosity between Eric and Wexford, pages 16–23.

For a contrast suggest *Reunion* by Fred Uhlman, which is about Hans Schwarz, son of a Jewish doctor, and Konradin von Hohenfels, son of an illustrious family, whose mother despises Jews. The two boys become fast friends even though Konradin has to fight for every minute he spends with Hans. The growth of anti-Semitism makes no difference to Konradin, and during World War II the young man lives up to his idealized conception of friendship.

Knox, Bill

The Hanging Tree.   1984.   Doubleday.

When two men hold up a small red Royal Mail van about to deliver pension money to a post office in a slum area of Glasgow and kill a young motorcyclist who inadvertently gets in their way, Detective Superintendent Colin Thane of the Scottish Crime Squad in Glasgow takes charge of the investigation. In his saddlebags, the dead young man, Ted Douglas, had three video copies of a new American movie that has not yet been released outside the United States. The thought is that organized crime probably has had a hand in the pirating of the film. Thane's two assistants, Detective Sergeant Francey Dunbar and Detective Constable Sandra Craig, do their share of legwork and research. They find little of interest in Douglas's apartment except that it is too well stocked for a man without a steady job. In the garage where Douglas kept his motorcycle, Thane and Dunbar find a gun, a passport under another name, and three thick bundles of bank notes hidden behind some bricks. Friends and neighbors of the dead man are questioned, and one of them mentions that Douglas had worked part-time for a firm called Falcon Services. When Thane goes out to question someone there, the dispatcher is not overly cordial or cooperative. Another lead is a tip to call on Joe Daisy, a street-level dealer in video tapes. Thane gives Joe his phone number in case the man later decides to give him information. One by one different leads come in and are followed up; each brings valuable information. It is finally decided that pirated video tapes are being made in Scotland and not near London. A place is pinpointed for attack, and the criminals are either killed or apprehended.

The author writes well, and his major characters seem like real people. Some of the laboratory reports are particularly interesting. The composition of the soil found on Douglas's boots and tires helps Thane to pinpoint the area where the young man had been. Eventually the police solve the crime through that information. The young people recommended this story.

In a booktalk tell briefly of the holdup, Thane and his team being assigned to the case, and the discovery of the money in

Douglas's garage, pages 1–3, 8–11, 22–23. This should be enough to awaken interest in reading the mystery.

In *Live Bait* by Knox, Colin Thane is on his first case as Detective Superintendent. A hit-and-run victim is identified as a possible member of a European drug ring, and with very little information at hand, Thane begins his investigation. When the case is solved, he finds himself proud of his new staff. In another mystery, *A Killing in Antiques*, Colin Thane discovers a group of men who burglarize the homes of people who have antiques. In *The Crossfire Killings* Thane finds there is a lot more to be uncovered in the death of Detective Sergeant May Dutton than its cause. Bill Knox has written another series of stories about Webb Carrick, first mate on Her Majesty's Fisheries Protection Service cruiser *Marlin*. In *Bloodtide* the body of a friend of the *Marlin*'s Captain Shannon, is found in the ice bunker on one of the fishing boats. Between them Carrick and Shannon solve the murder and also uncover a drug-smuggling ring. *Wavecrest* stars Carrick in command of his own ship. Two bodies with pieces of a boat are found in the ocean, and the boat-repair yard and its foreman at a nearby port are destroyed by fire. These events give Carrick and his crew plenty of action in solving the mystery. Mature readers may be introduced to *Death of an Expert Witness* by P. D. James. Dr. Lorrimer, senior biologist at Hoggatt's Forensic Science Laboratory, is found brutally murdered in a triply locked building with an electronic warning system connected to the local police station. Commander Adam Dalgleish and Detective Inspector John Massingham are assigned to what seems at first an unsolvable case. *Death in the Greenhouse* by John R. L. Anderson is a well written, well planned tale of a mysterious death, in which no clues point to the murderer. Col. Peter Blair, a meticulous, very sensitive, and competent investigator, is asked to work on the case and brings it to a plausible conclusion.

Kurtis, Bill

Bill Kurtis on Assignment. 1983. Rand-McNally.

While acting as anchorman for WBBM-TV in Chicago, Kurtis begins traveling to areas that are making headlines. He wants to gather details that will add a new level of public understanding of the events. In 1980 a Chicago doctor, who is an Iranian, offers to guide him to what will be an inside picture of the situation in Iran when that country is holding hostage sixty Americans from the U.S. Embassy. A cameraman and a sound technician accompany Kurtis. The reader gets quite a different picture of Iran and a better understanding of the situation there after reading the opening chapter. Agent Orange, a defoliant used by the United States in Vietnam, is a term familiar to most people who listen to the news on radio or television or read a newspaper. Kurtis and his crew go to Vietnam where he sees the barren areas where Agent Orange has been used. He interviews people who have been involved in the war and investigates the use of similar chemicals here in the United States. There is no question in his mind that the U.S. government has allowed the use of inadequately tested chemicals both here and abroad. His stay in Vietnam arouses his interest in the many Amerasian children and the Asian children orphaned by the war. Kurtis records what he calls his most frightening but also most exhilarating experience—his flight on a plane carrying rice to the beseiged city of Phnom Penh. In 1981 he goes to El Salvador to try to get the true story behind the headlines in American newspapers. His story makes one question the United States position in Central America today. He does investigative reporting on wildlife in Africa and Asia that results in a two-hour-long broadcast entitled "Passport to Extinction" in which he tells how animals, birds, and reptiles are being slaughtered in or exported illegally from these areas. The final chapter concerns Poland, the growth of Solidarity, and its suppression. Each chapter contains black-and-white photographs, and there are two sections of dramatic photographs in color.

Kurtis writes succinctly and well, as might be expected of a reporter and broadcaster. Many junior high students seemed uninterested in the book, but it does have appeal for young people who would like to be writers or reporters, whether or not they have a connection with television.

Any one of the chapters could be used in a booktalk.

With the help of Mickey Hershowitz, Dan Rather wrote his autobiography, *The Camera Never Blinks,* in the 1970s. He got his start on radio when he was in college in Texas and gradually climbed the ladder of success because he was forthright and had a sense of obligation to tell the truth as he actually saw it. Young people considering journalism as a career might also want to think about Charles Kuralt's brand of writing and interviewing. *On the Road with Charles Kuralt* brings together the best of his work. In *The Flight of the Condor* Michael Andrews, a producer for the BBC, tells of getting the photographs and information on the unusual flora and fauna of the Andes from Cape Horn north to the equator and the rain forest of the Amazon. This is recommended for those to whom exploration appeals.

Lanier, Sterling E.

Hiero's Journey. 1983. Ballantine.

Five thousand years after The Death (nuclear destruction), Abbot Demero of the Metz Republic in western Canada sends Hiero, a warrior-priest, to the area south of the Inland Sea (the Great Lakes) to learn if a computer or instructions for building one still exist. The abbot needs a computer in order to find a way to destroy the Unclean, a dark brotherhood that seeks to destroy humanity. Hiero sets out on his telepathically controlled horse, Klootz. A bit later a young bear named Gorm joins Hiero, who finds he can also communicate with the bear mentally. Fierce beasts sent by the Unclean often pursue them and are beaten off. Early in the book Hiero rescues Luchare, a slave girl, from being killed by giant birds. She has fled from her father's kingdom because she refuses to marry the man her father has chosen. After days of travel, disaster strikes suddenly. Realizing they have been ambushed, Hiero drops from the saddle and orders Klootz, Gorm, and Luchare to retreat to safety. Before he can fire, he is hit in the chest and knocked unconscious by a missile that strikes the cross hanging around his neck; luckily he is only bruised. He is imprisoned on Dead Isle but, by using his mind powers, he escapes, miraculously overcoming every obstacle in his way to rejoin Luchare and the animals. They continue their journey, and days later are caught on an island by the Unclean. There is no way they can escape. Then suddenly a canoe bearing an old man comes in sight. He is an Elevener, thus named because of his group's support of the eleventh commandment, "Thou shalt not destroy the earth nor the life thereon." His power over animals completely destroys the Unclean attackers. He tells them that he wishes to join them and that he has a ship waiting a short distance away. More danger awaits them, and again they escape. Eventually they discover a great cavern equipped with engines, machinery, a control board, and other strange devices. Here Luchare finds three volumes entitled "Principles of a Basic Analog Computer," which she carries with her when they escape the cavern before it blows up, killing all their enemies who have followed them.

The story is not only about the destruction of evil by the forces of good but also is of interest because it shows how remnants of the human race can make a comeback after a holocaust and begin to rebuild. Man was the most intelligent creature to evolve when life on earth began originally, and it is worthy of note that other forms of animal life increased their mental capacity after The Death. The characters are interesting, and the author's imagination has created many forms for evil to assume. The junior high readers liked the book very much.

For a booktalk pages 21–29 can be used to give some background information about survivors from the holocaust and to tell what Hiero is expected to do on his journey south. This may be enough, but the speaker can also add some facts about Klootz and Gorm from chapter 1.

Also recommend *The Unforsaken Hiero,* in which Hiero is spirited away from his father-in-law's household by two followers of the Unclean. By accident he escapes death and goes on to more adventures. A gigantic snail with an interesting history heals most of the mind damage the Unclean have done to Hiero with drugs, helping him greatly to protect himself on his dangerous journey. The Unclean cause him much more trouble, but Hiero wins in the end. After a short nuclear war, a three-year winter, and years of epidemics, Gordon Krantz starts from Minnesota to walk west. In eastern Oregon he comes upon a dead mailman in a rusted jeep and takes the skeleton's clothing, shoes, and mailbag. Prior to this he has earned his keep by entertaining in settlements along the way. Now he says that the government is beginning to establish itself in St. Paul City and that he is the official who has come to set up post offices. Hence, the title David Brin chose for his novel, *The Postman.* Eventually Gordon becomes a leader in combatting radicals who live like feudal lords. This is probably too adult for most junior high readers. Try it with average senior high students. *Fate of the Earth* by Jonathan Schnell and *The Cold and the Dark* by Paul Ehrlich and others present modern scientists' views of what a holocaust could do to life on earth.

Lee, Harper

To Kill a Mockingbird. 1960. Lippincott.

This is an unsentimental account of life in the small town of Maycomb, Alabama, in the 1930s. It is especially the story of one family, the Finches. The father, Atticus, is a lawyer and legislator; the son Jem is ten; and Jean Louise, more commonly known as Scout, is the tomboy younger sister. When Atticus is at the office or out of town, Calpurnia, the black cook, looks after the children, whose mother is dead. With Scout as narrator, a picture of the people and way of life emerges. Most of the book centers around the adventures of the children and their friend Dill, who comes to Maycomb during vacations. They are very curious about Boo Radley, a recluse neighbor who has not been outside his home for many years, and the youngsters have several escapades attempting to find out about this man whom they have never seen. To the dismay of his neighbors and friends, Atticus, appointed to defend a young black, Tom Robinson, who has been accused of raping Mayella Ewell, a girl from the town's most disreputable white family, decides that the man is innocent and goes all out to prove it. When a group threatens to lynch Tom, Atticus attempts to protect him, but it is Scout who actually saves the day. The children see abuse heaped upon themselves and their father as a result of his stand. Against their father's orders, Jem and Scout go to the courthouse to watch the trial. Friendly blacks let them sit in their section, and through Scout's eyes the reader witnesses the trial. Although Tom is convicted, the jury does deliberate outside the courtroom for hours, and a number of people in town feel that he is innocent. Mayella's father, trying to get even with Atticus for showing him up as a liar, tries to kill Jem and Scout, but Boo Radley, who has always watched the children, saves them.

Good readers from junior high up are enthusiastic about this book. It has a quiet style, but the picture of family life through Scout's eyes is very appealing. The trial is excellently handled without sensationalism. It is not the charge of rape that is important but the fact that prejudice is operating to ruin the life of a human being. This discovery makes a great impression on Jem, and when he finds it disturbing, Atticus tries to explain it so that the boy sees the event in its proper perspective. The manner in which Atticus and Calpurnia handle many different events as the children are growing up shows how values can be instilled in the younger generation by patience, understanding, and discipline, coupled with common sense.

Booktalks can be based on the occasion when Walter Cunningham comes home to lunch with Scout, pages 25–31, and the incident in which Jem ruins Mrs. Dubose's camellias, pages 108–21.

Serious readers who want more information about life in the South will agonize with Anne Moody in her autobiography, *Coming of Age in Mississippi*, in which she describes her life as a black in the Deep South between 1940 and 1964. She has used some four-letter words and some profanity, but her book is a stirring, dramatic portrait. See also *Black Like Me*° by John Griffin. In *The Member of the Wedding* by Carson McCullers, twelve-year-old Francie Addams is also a motherless child in the Deep South. Her closest friend is Berenice, the black cook. Her father pays little attention to her, and her friends have matured more quickly than she has. They ignore her. The story takes place during summer vacation, and it is a painful time for Francie. Nothing goes right, and even her fantasies have a bitter ending. This is quite a contrast to the family in *To Kill a Mockingbird*.

Lord, Walter

A Night to Remember.   1955.   Holt.

When Walter Lord was ten years of age, he persuaded his parents to make their trip to Europe on the *Olympia*, sister ship of the *Titanic*, so that he could learn as much as possible about the liner. He spent a good part of the next twenty-eight years in careful research, talking or corresponding with survivors and relatives of passengers and reading reports of the sinking. As a result, this book is a graphic description of the events and the passengers on the night the *Titanic* rams an iceberg and sinks. The story begins on April 14, 1912, at 11:40 P.M. on the fifth night of the ship's maiden voyage. A few minutes later the ship strikes the iceberg. The few first-class passengers who realize what has happened are unperturbed because they know that the *Titanic* is unsinkable. But down in steerage, in the crew's quarters, in the postal department, and in the boiler room, the reaction is different. Water rushes in, forcing the crew and passengers to scramble for safety. Meanwhile, the captain and the liner's builder have figured the ship's chances for survival, and orders go out to get the people quietly into the lifeboats, which can carry only 1,178 of the 2,207 persons aboard. The wireless operator sends out the CQD call to summon help. The *California*, which is only ten miles away and warned the big ship of icebergs earlier in the evening, has stopped her engines, being surrounded by drifting ice. All but her watch had retired. At 12:25 A.M. the *Carpathia*, fifty-eight miles away, picks up the distress signal and immediately changes course, racing to help. The descriptions of the loading of the *Titanic*'s lifeboats and of the preparations for rescue aboard the *Carpathia* are both thrilling and chilling. As a result of this disaster in which 1,400 lives were lost, many changes were made in the safety requirements for passenger ships in an effort to ward off similar tragedies in the future.

This book seems to appeal to readers from junior high up.

A summary similar to the foregoing is usually enough to interest readers in the book.

In *The Night Lives on,* Lord gives further information about the *Titanic*'s passengers and the sinking, clears up some of the mysteries, and includes the finding of the ship in 1985. For other stories of disaster at sea, suggest *Saved! The Story of the Andrea Doria.* Also, *Beyond Reach: The Search for the Titanic* by William Hoffman is an account of the 1981 search for the *Titanic* and includes a discussion of other books about the disaster and a brief mention of other ships that have sunk. *The Morro Castle* by Hal Burton describes the destruction of a beautiful cruise ship by fire and a great loss of life. *Abandon Ship* by Richard Newcombe relates the sinking of the heavy cruiser USS *Indianapolis* by the Japanese in 1945. *The Perilous Seas,* edited by Clarrisa Silitch, includes true stories of disasters or of dramatic rescue attempts of persons on small vessels, ocean liners, and navy ships in peacetime and in war. The earliest takes place in the War of 1812 but most are much more recent, the latest happening in 1979. In *Sole Survivor,* Ruthanne Lum McCunn describes the harrowing experiences of Poon Lim, a Chinese lad who had worked on *Benlomond,* a cargo ship that was torpedoed and sunk by a German submarine. Lim, the only survivor, manages to climb aboard a loose life raft on which he lives for 133 days before drifting to the mouth of the Amazon River.

Lose, M. Phyllis

No Job for a Lady, as told to Daniel Mannix.   1979. Macmillan.

From the time she is three, Phyllis Lose is fascinated by horses, but it isn't until she is ten that she has a pony, which she gladly shares with her sisters and brother. She spends a lot of time watching, listening, and learning at the Four Horsemen Riding Club, where the pony is boarded. One day Phyllis discovers a deserted barn and proposes to her father that they rent the barn and board horses themselves. He agrees, and the whole family pitches in to make it a success. Phyllis especially learns a great deal and makes some valuable friends, among them a blacksmith and a veterinarian. No one can discourage her when she decided to become a veterinarian herself, even though it will take nine years to finish her schooling. To earn money for college she exercises horses for a couple of stables and rides horses in shows. The book is packed with episodes from her experiences riding and working with horses. In 1957 she graduates from veterinary school and passes the state boards, getting her license to practice. People have little confidence in a woman veterinarian at the time, but gradually she builds a clientele. She describes many very interesting calls she has to make in all kinds of weather and at all times of day and night. She eventually becomes veterinarian for several important private stables and also takes care of all the horses and dogs used by the Philadelphia Police Department. There comes a time when she is able to build her own hospital for horse patients. Her family is very close, and after Phyllis begins practicing, her father handles her finances, and her mother and sister act as drivers, secretaries, and schedulers.

Once readers begin this book, they find it difficult to put down before it is finished. The author certainly shows what determination, intelligence, and hard work can accomplish.

The first incident in the book, telling of a call to help a mare having difficulty delivering its foal, shows how the family cooperated to help Phyllis and how she carried on her work, often under great difficulty. This can be used as a booktalk, pages 3–13.

More women are entering types of work traditionally reserved for men. The following books are suggested for girls interested in these kinds of occupations. Margaret Bourke-White began by developing industrial advertising through photographs and later was at many fronts during World War II in Europe. Toward the end of her career she covered trouble in South Africa and India and the war in Korea. Unfortunately her own autobiography, *Portrait of Myself,* is out of print, but Jonathan Silverman in *For the World to See: The Life of Margaret Bourke-White* quotes often from her writings and includes many of her outstanding photographs. It is only in the last twenty years that a significant number of women have voluntarily lived and worked in wilderness areas. Anne LaBastille, in *Women and Wilderness,* profiles fifteen women who have preferred to make their living in the wilds of Alaska, the tropical forest of Surinam, the plains of Africa, the reefs of the Red Sea, or the caves of some Caribbean areas. Over the years teens have enjoyed books by Eugenie Clark and Margaret Murie, two of the women included. LaBastille told of her own wilderness experiences in *Woodswoman* and *Assignment: Wildlife,* listed in *Doors to More Mature Reading,* second edition. *The Work of Her Hands,* a novel by Anne Knowles, is a nice love story about a young woman in England who became a veterinarian. Her story is continued in *An Ark on the Flood;* she is now married to a veterinarian, and the couple's experiences on the job and with the people of the Milchester area provide humor, excitement, and human and animal interest and also portray a nice husband-and-wife relationship. In *Women in*

War Shelley Saywell describes women fighting during World War II, mostly in the underground. The first chapter, on women pilots in England, is the least exciting because they did not fight; although there was certainly danger in flying newly made planes in all kinds of weather to the fields where men were waiting to use them against the Germans. Women fought in the army or underground in France, Italy, Poland, Russia, Palestine, and Indochina. Most recently they have been involved in Vietnam, the Falklands, and El Salvador.

Lund, Doris

Patchwork Clan. 1982. Little, Brown.

Katherine Ann Taylor was an only child, and because she was not a well youngster, she had to spend many lonely hours in bed. She took lessons on the piano and cello and was a music major in college. Before she graduated, she married a boy she had known since high school. By the time she is twenty-five, however, she is a divorcee with three small children she supports by giving piano lessons. She also plays the cello in an orchestra where she falls in love with John Sweeny, the conductor. They marry and in time have two children of their own. When Ann loses her sixth child in a miscarriage, she is badly upset. She and her husband finally decide to adopt a child, and so Marcus comes into their lives. He is a mixture of black, American Indian, and possibly German or Scotch-Irish, six months old, with flaming red hair. He is such an engaging little fellow that they apply for another baby. While they are waiting for that one, Ann produces twins herself, and when they are ten months old, the second adoption comes through. This child was a girl with honey skin, tight dark curls, and great topaz eyes, the child of a white mother and a black father. Then a beautiful black baby boy is added, almost the same age as the little girl. Thus it appears as if the parents have two sets of twins. Later a Vietnamese teenager and a blind Indian child from South America join the family. A great deal of the narrative concerns the last three children to be adopted, who are survivors of a well-off Vietnamese family that had fled the enemy approaching Saigon. Chuong, carrying the baby, manages to get on a fishing boat that eventually reaches Hong Kong. He finds his little brother on the boat but never sees the rest of the family again. The author describes her unusual family's everyday life and problems and its special celebrations.

This thoroughly enjoyable story is very easy to read, has some tense moments, and furnishes quite a few laughs.

The three Vietnamese children are brought for a two-day visit so that the Sweenys can see whether they really want to adopt all three. Pages 30–60 tell of the visit, and there are numerous other incidents that could be woven into a booktalk.

Joseph Blank in *19 Steps up the Mountain* tells the courageous and moving story of Dorothy and Tom Atwood and the children they adopted, a number of them severely handicapped. Although *Tony: Our Journey Together* by Carolyn Koons is not about a large family, it is concerned with serious family problems. Tony is put in prison in Mexico when he is only five years of age. He is eleven when the author adopts him and he becomes a citizen of the United States. Then the problems begin because Tony has been on his own for a long time and has had rough treatment. It is some time before he can adjust to a safe, loving home and freedom with discipline.

MacAvoy, R. A.

Tea with the Black Dragon. 1983. Bantam.

Martha MacNamara's daughter, Elizabeth, has sent for her to come to California and has reserved a room for her at the swank James Herald Hotel in San Francisco. It is there that Martha meets Mayland Long, an Oriental gentleman. Mr. Long has an old recording that Martha made before she gave up her career as a violinist to marry and have a child. He is not a musician, but he does appreciate fine music, and he invites her to have dinner with him the next evening. Martha expected to see her daughter, Liz, that day but has not even had a call from her. When Martha calls Liz's place of employment, she learns that her daughter no longer works there. Long offers to help her look for Liz. They check Liz's place of employment to see if anyone there knows where she has gone. Then they try Stanford University but without luck. Long guides her to a shop called Friendly Computers run by a young man about Liz's age, who Long thinks might know something, but he is no help. As Martha and Mr. Long walk toward her hotel, they are separated for a minute, and Martha reaches the crossing before he does. A bus pulls to the curb after she has crossed in front of it, and when Long follows, she has disappeared. She is not in the lobby or in her room; she is gone. He calls the police, who tell him a day has to elapse before she can be regarded as missing. Long goes to see Liz's boss, Floyd Rasmussen, but he cannot help. Late that afternoon Long returns to the building where Rasmussen has his office; he has decided to follow the man and finds an inconspicuous place to stand and watch. Soon there emerges a tall blonde who looks enough like Martha to be her daughter, and he follows her home. It takes some time before she is convinced that he is only interested in finding her mother, but she finally tells him that a way has been discovered to make a fortune by creating corporate dummy accounts at a bank, and she knows who has done it. Martha has been kidnapped to keep Liz silent until the culprits make their escape. Long manages to save both Martha and Liz.

This is a fantasy with a difference. Mayland had once been an imperial black Chinese dragon. Somehow he has been turned into an Oriental gentleman who still has magical powers when he needs them, but the reader doesn't know this until late in the story. When he falls in love with Martha, nothing can keep him from doing all he can to help her in her desperate situation.

In a booktalk introduce Martha and Mayland and tell how he goes with her while she tries to locate her daughter. Then describe how she disappears, pages 1–13, 46–47.

Also suggest *The Chinese Bell Murders* by Robert van Gulik, in which Judge Dee, famous in Chinese popular literature, not only acts as a detective to solve murders in three separate cases but also gives typically grizzly sentences to the defendants he tries in court.

McConnell, Malcolm

Into the Mouth of the Cat: The Story of Lance Sijan, Hero of Vietnam. 1985. Norton.

When Lance Sijan was growing up in Milwaukee, Wisconsin, he was all-city captain in football and president of the student council as well as a star in several high school theatrical productions. After graduating from the Air Force Academy, he took his final F-4 training and was sent to the

Philippines for jungle survival training. Later, in 1967, he joins a combat wing in Vietnam. On November 9 he is flying as backseater to the squadron's commanding officer. As the plane makes its bombing attack, the bombs—instead of dropping—detonate just as they leave the plane, and the plane explodes. Lance ejects, his parachute opens, and he lands on the top of a heavily forested karst in Laos about three miles from the target. He has a compound fracture of his left leg, a hole in his head, a concussion, and a badly mangled hand. As soon as he is able, he uses his morphine syringes and sulfa powder before applying a sterile battle dressing to his leg. The next morning he manages to talk to the rescue commander by radio, but ground fire makes it difficult for the planes to determine his exact position. Very late in the day one Green Giant gets close enough to let down its penetrator, but it is a distance away. Lance has to put his radio in a pocket to crawl, and before he reaches the lift, the helicopter has to withdraw because of enemy fire. In getting back to his water bottles and pistol, he drops into a limestone sinkhole and passes out. The next day the rescue team comes early, but since Lance does not answer their radio call, they give up, thinking he has died. When he comes to, he does not know how long he has been unconscious, as his watch is broken. He was eventually captured and placed in a hut with a guard whom he tricked, using a karati chop and escaped. He knows he has to move slowly because his back and hips are raw where his suit has been torn away by the rocks. By the time he is recaptured, two other pilots have been shot down and captured. Although these men do all they can to care for Lance, he dies, but not before telling in detail about his weeks alone in the jungle.

This is a harrowing story because readers can clearly picture what Lance went through day after day, but it is also suspenseful because readers feel that Lance will actually get back to his own people. It is difficult to see how he could have endured such hardship and not have his spirit crushed. His family throws light on this part of the narrative. The author, who attended the same high school as Lance, now teaches journalism and fiction writing. He has written an excellent account of an American hero's life.

A booktalker can identify Lance and then, using pages 61–62, 69–72, and 95–99, tell about the plane's exploding and the rescue attempt. The intervening pages give many details but are not necessary for a booktalk.

Boys who like *Raspberry One*, a juvenile story by Charles Ferry concerning two nineteen-year-old members of the crew of a Navy torpedo bomber assigned to the aircraft carrier *Shiloh* and the hell they endure in helping take Iwo Jima and Okinawa from the Japanese can be introduced to McConnell. Shot down over Laos, Dieter Dengler, who tells his story in *Escape from Laos*, is not as badly injured as Lance and eludes the enemy for a short time. Captured and often mistreated, he ends up in a jungle prison camp with several other American flyers. Eventually they split into teams and escape. In *Phantom over Vietnam* ex–Marine Corps pilot John Trotti takes the reader with him on missions against the enemy, detailing not only every move the pilot makes but also the communication with other planes, helicopters, and ground crew. Trotti completed over 600 missions on two tours of duty and also spent two and a half years as an instructor in the United States.

McCracken, Mary

Turnabout Children.   1986.   Little, Brown.

In describing her work with children who have learning disabilities, the author reports on five who came to her for help. Blessed with a sense of humor, a good vocabulary, practical judgment, and common sense, Joey has an appealing personality and is bright, but he gets letters and numbers mixed up and is more active, tense, and distracted than the usual seven-year-old. Mary works with him on reading, writing, and arithmetic all summer, and in the fall he is placed in second grade with an experienced, very demanding teacher with whom Mary can work. Between them Joey improves in his schoolwork, but the next year, under a new, inexperienced teacher, Joey is lost again. Though tragedy at home adds to his disturbed mental state, Mary is able to straighten things out partially. When a new teacher takes over after Christmas, Joey shows improvement and eventually is able to graduate with his class. Eric, who cannot form words, is a very interesting, quite different case. He is making progress, but some family problems force the boy's mother to leave the area with him. Mary never hears from them again. From a well-to-do family, twelve-year-old Ben is completely defeated and downcast, but Mary has a way of reaching children. She tells about every test she administers to Ben. He scores above the average range of intelligence, but his academic achievement is way below; for example, he does not know the months of the year, but he can answer in detail a question about hieroglyphics. Mary helps him. Alice has attended a private school before her family moved to the East Coast but now goes to a public school with high academic achievement. Arithmetic is one of her main difficulties. When Mary explains the basic elements, Alice catches on quickly, but she has difficulty with visual-motor tasks. It is not easy for her to write and align numbers, and she can remember only one number at a time. These problems are solved. When Charlie comes to Mary for the first time, he brings a large piece of paper containing a drawing and a story. For "again" he has written "apen," for "wreck" he has "retk," for "evacuating" he has "vakuwede." In measured reasoning, abstract thinking, and spatial relationships he is superior, but his rote memory is very poor. He cannot match letters and sounds. If four directions are given at once, he has no idea what to do. Mary explains how the problems can be overcome, and they get busy.

This book's best use is with young people who have read other books by Mary and by Tony Hayden* and want more information about methods used in working with problem children.

Turnabout Children can be used in a booktalk if the potential readers are familiar with the easier books; otherwise lead up to this one with the ones suggested below.

In *Lovey* Mary tells how she coped with the screaming, angry, and dirty Hannah. The eight-year-old is assigned to Mary's schoolroom, where she already has three emotionally disturbed boys who need all her attention. When the school where Mary works becomes accredited, she is dismissed because she does not have a degree, and she decides to go to the university and finish her education. While she does this, she works with several problem children. The first is Luke— small, only seven, but with twenty-four arrests for arson, theft, and truancy. This book is *City Kid*.

MacDonald, Ervin Austin

The Rainbow Chasers.   1982.   Salem House.

In 1868 Canadian Archie MacDonald leaves the family farm and business to try to make his fortune prospecting. Although he finds some minerals, he never makes a fortune. When he is working at a mine, he meets and marries Mary Prouty, and they soon move to a homestead where Archie buys and sells cattle and horses. He and Mary have five children, two girls and three boys. Mary dies shortly after the birth of a fourth son, who also dies. The children have to be placed in an orphanage because Archie cannot take care of them and work on the farm. When his son Ervin (the author) is nine, Archie takes them home for the summer, and they learn to do farm work, but in the fall they return to the orphanage. Finally in 1905 Archie sells the farm and takes the boys with him to a homestead southeast of Edmonton. Here they work harder than they have ever worked before—preparing the land for planting, seeding, haying, harvesting, building a house and outbuildings, fencing, and fighting a prairie fire. After a couple of years Archie sells the place and, with the boys and a pack train, sets out for the Cariboo across the Rockies in British Columbia. For nearly four months Archie leads them over the roughest, most difficult trail imaginable, and then one day they come out of the pines into a sidehill with a clear view. At the bottom of the hill is a beautiful lake surrounded by many acres of waving grass. They all know this is the spot for which they have been looking. They are able to buy some land. The ingenuity of the boys and their father in establishing a home here and preparing for winter is amazing. The author, only fourteen years old at the time, stays at the larger cabin alone all winter. Every few weeks he takes fresh bread he has baked and some milk over to his dad and two brothers in a cabin on the meadow. One year they lose most of their draft horses to a virus and another time a terrible late blizzard destroys most of a just-purchased herd of range cattle. He recounts experiences on the trap line in the dead of winter with the frigid temperature once as low as sixty degrees below zero. When Archie dies in 1929, the boys, who are all married by this time, sell the ranch because they can't make enough to support three families.

Reading this book can be compared to listening to a good storyteller describing the many adventures in his life. There is almost no conversation. The author's experiences are exciting, humorous, unusual, sometimes almost unbelievable, and sad—in other words, simply fascinating for those who love adventure.

There are countless episodes for booktalks. A French-Canadian agrees to buy a fat steer from Archie once a week until his construction job is finished, and then he refuses to pay, pages 35–36. When Archie plans to take Angus with him to find a new farm, he puts Dan and Ervin in a Catholic mission school, pages 65–68, 79. Lost in a blizzard, pages 76–77; fighting a prairie fire, pages 87–89; watering the cattle and horses in subzero temperatures, pages 91–92; Archie's dream about the new ranch in British Columbia, pages 94–98; a list of supplies for the three boys and their father for crossing the mountains, page 102; Ervin explaining about his cooking on the trail, pages 110–12; and Dan finding a bag of money, pages 169–71, are other possibilities.

Ruffles on My Longjohns by Isabel Edwards seems a natural follow-up. It is the true story of the author and her husband, who homestead in British Columbia. She recounts the highlights of their years there—the humorous, dangerous, frightening, and delightful ones—in her book. In *Giants in the Earth* by Ole Rolvaag, Per Hansa with his wife and three children stake out a claim in Dakota Territory and labor long hours to establish a home. Because of his determination and resourcefulness, they do better than their neighbors, but the story has a sad ending. It takes some maturity on the part of teenagers to appreciate this classic tale of American pioneer life.

Mackal, Roy P.

Searching for Hidden Animals. 1980. Doubleday.

Mackal, a biochemist and zoologist at the University of Chicago, has inquired into zoological mysteries and the existence of strange animals, most of which are thought to be extinct. However, the author wonders if some of these creatures may still survive in remote areas. He begins with research done in Arctic waters in 1741 by Georg Wilhelm Steller, who observed an animal he called a sea ape but was unable to capture it. Steller prepared a complete skeleton of another animal new to scientists, the sea cow, but because of circumstances beyond his control, he could not bring the skeleton home. Mackal thinks that this animal may still be found in the very far north. He discusses sea serpents and the leopard seal and wonders whether or not Steller's sea ape could have been a juvenile leopard seal. The author believes that there are giant octopuses even though some scientists say that sightings have been of giant squid, not of octopuses. On November 30, 1896, a giant carcass was found on the beach at St. Augustine, Florida. It was not identified for many years because the tentacles were missing and the carcass was in bad condition. More recently a scientist was able to obtain a piece of the animal, which had been preserved in formaldehyde at the Smithsonian Institution. Under the microscope, the creature was identified as an octopus. The coelacanth, the ancient fish that is a living example of the ancestors of vertebrates, was discovered fairly recently in Africa. Lack of funds has prevented much research in Africa, and Mackal believes there are unknown animals there. He discusses the Buru, probably a giant lizard, that once existed in a valley in the Himalayas; no research has been done there. He also discusses the extinct Dodo, a flightless bird. The author ends his study by telling of monsters sighted in lakes in the United States and Canada. Only a few of the reports on these give enough detail for an identification to be made. The last chapter considers monstrous plants.

Mackal writes very well and has aimed his book at the general reader, not the specialist. He has done a good deal of research in connection with the Loch Ness monster, so he has the background for writing about zoological mysteries. There is need for such research, and young people just might become interested in pursuing study in these areas.

Chapter 5 concerns the Buru and could be used in a booktalk. It describes the coming of the natives to the valley and the competition between people draining the swamps to create more farmland and the Buru, aquatic vegetarians that live in the swamps.

Robert F. Burgess, in *Secret Languages of the Sea*, writes about the research by outstanding scientists that has disclosed many previously unknown and astonishing facts about creatures of the sea. In *Ark on the Move,* which is illustrated with lovely color photographs, Gerald Durrell describes the unusual animals, birds, flowers, and trees that his group found on the islands of Mauritius, Rodrigues, and Madagascar.

Marshall, Catherine

Julie.   1984.   McGraw-Hill.

In 1934 the Wallace family moves to Alderton, Pennsylvania, where the father has bought the town's weekly newspaper. Alderton is an industrial town with a steel mill, a wire plant, and railroad yards; employees are paid minimal wages, live in shacks built by the employers, and trade at employer-owned stores. A union is just beginning to try to organize the workers. The whole Wallace family has to work to publish the newspaper because they can barely afford their one employee. Julie, in her last year in high school, is the proofreader, while young Tim and Anna Marie fold and deliver the paper and do odd jobs around the office. Almost immediately after Mr. Wallace takes over the paper, Dean Fleming, a retired railroad man, comes in and volunteers to keep the old press in running order, free of charge. He says he has a feeling that he has been sent to do it. Interested in journalism, Julie is soon trying her skill at writing for the paper, and her father sometimes uses an article. Narrated by Julie, the story includes her school and dating experiences as well as information about the paper. One of her first acquaintances is a young Englishman who manages the Fishing and Hunting Club on Lake Kassawha, a private body of water behind a large earthen dam. Julie and her best friend Margo go out to the club with a picnic lunch one Saturday, and he answers many questions about the dam for Julie. She later tells her father that the dam gives her a feeling of danger, but at first her father laughs off her premonition. In December he tells the family the paper will have to fold: they are entirely out of money, and the bank will not give him a loan. Just then Dean Fleming presents Mr. Wallace with a check for $500. It isn't until the paper begins to take a stand in the union situation and, eventually, on the safety of the dam that business begins to pick up. The high point of the story is

112

the collapse of the dam and the disaster that strikes Alderton.

The character development traced in both Julie and her father is splendid. Julie matures quickly under the conditions in which she is placed; her father grows in strength of body and character under the influence of Dean Fleming, a strong Christian man. Anyone who has read a book about the Johnstown flood will recognize that the events before and during the Alderton flood are similar. The girls in my group liked the book very much.

The fact that Julie falls flat in the mud just as she meets the handsome Englishman for the first time should interest many girls, pages 3–7. He is not the only romantic interest. The new young minister falls in love with Julie, as does one of the boys in her class at school.

Those who have not read *Christy* by Catherine Marshall should be introduced to it. Christy at age nineteen goes to Cutter Gap in the Great Smoky Mountains to teach school in 1912. In this isolated community the people are very poor and still living in the eighteenth century. Tragedies that occur upset Christy, and there seems little she can do to improve matters, but an old Quaker lady helps Christy find peace of mind, and in the end she also finds her true love. Another family story in which a teenage girl plays a leading role is *The State of Stony Lonesome* by Jessamyn West. Ginerva has a good deal of responsibility in her home, and it seems at times that she is not really appreciated for her diligence. However, a beloved uncle recognizes her virtues and, in time, the family also does.

Mebane, Mary E.

Mary. 1981. Viking.

Born in 1933, Mary Mebane lives on a small farm in Durham County, North Carolina. Her mother works in a tobacco factory, and her father earns what he can collecting trash. The land is poor but good enough to raise vegetables that they either sell or can for winter use. When Mary is very small and discovering new things every day, she thinks life is wonderful. Then she realizes that her mother does not like her, but she never learns the reason. When she starts school, she is puzzled by many unfamiliar words, but she is bright and

113

soon catches on. As the years go by, she wins several awards, but she never mentions them at home because she knows the family is not interested. As soon as she is allowed to use the school library, she hurries through her assignments so that she can read books. She soon realizes that her education is not as good as that received by the white students in their school. She wants to be somebody but doesn't know how she could be. Her family does have a piano, so she goes to the best black piano teacher and offers to work for her in return for lessons. Perhaps she can be a concert pianist. Her Aunt Jo, who lives with the family, encourages her. After her father dies, her brothers go from bad to worse, and Aunt Jo leaves. Mary writes of the natural talent of many young blacks she knows who had no opportunity to make anything of it. She also tells of the effects of segregation. She is determined to go to college, and when Aunt Jo dies, she leaves Mary $600 toward further education. Mary is able to attend the college for blacks in Durham, although her mother disapproves strenuously. She comments on discrimination even among blacks: she is very dark, and the lighter-skinned blacks look down on her. To their surprise she graduates at the head of her class with a summa cum laude.

Mary Mebane does not tell what use she made of her education and how she escaped the fate of a black girl in the South. The book jacket says that she did earn an M.A. and a Ph.D. at the University of North Carolina in Chapel Hill. She has written for the *New York Times* and other publications and is currently teaching at the University of Wisconsin at Milwaukee.

The author has a meaningful way with words, and she draws the reader into her confrontations with her mother and brothers and into her dreams of a better life. She tells of the sordid lives of her contemporaries, many of whom live in poverty with a roving husband, bearing a baby every year. She worked until she achieved something better for herself. Her descriptions of events, people, and places are vividly drawn.

In a booktalk, the speaker can use some small happenings to show what kind of child Mary was. A neighbor wants to borrow a cup of sugar, pages 27–28; washdays, pages 12–14; first day at school, pages 38–39; a gift for Aunt Claudia, pages 47–49; and winning a contest on current events, pages 66–67 are just a few.

114

Another engrossing story of a black woman is *Marva Collins' Way* by Marva Collins and Civia Tamarkin. Dissatisfied with the methods used for teaching children in the public schools and convinced that her methods pay greater dividends, Mrs. Collins starts her own school, taking as pupils children who have been labeled retarded, emotionally disturbed, or hyperactive. In a very short time, Collins turns them into enthusiastic learners. Not all teenagers will wade through *Barbara Jordan: A Self-Portrait* by Barbara Jordan and Shelby Hearon, but those who do will definitely find it worth their time. Jordan is a person of whom all Americans can be proud and from whom they can learn a great deal. *Lena: A Personal and Professional Biography of Lena Horne* by James Haskins tells of the struggles of a beautiful black woman to make a name for herself as a singer and actress. She is beset by many family problems and by the prejudice of the white community against blacks appearing as entertainers in places reserved for white patrons. Another true account of a daughter of a poor black family in the Deep South is *You May Plow Here* by Thordis Simonsen. Though Sara Brooks has a strict but loving family, she, unlike Mary Mebane, does not have the urge to get an education and make something of herself when she is young. She struggles in poverty for many years before she gets a break during World War II and can acquire a home of her own and help her family. Her attitude and philosophy of life are particularly appealing.

Miller, Robert M.

Most of My Patients Are Animals.   1985.   Eriksson.

In childhood and adolescence, Robert Miller enthusiastically read books about animals, both domestic and wild. After fighting in World War II, he entered college to study animal husbandry and eventually became a doctor of veterinary medicine, married a girl he met in college, and set up a small home in a locality where he could gain experience as a veterinarian. In a short time they moved to the Conejo Valley in California, where he now has an animal hospital that serves both tame and wild animals. Veterinarians are on call twenty-four hours a day, and Miller has packed his account with experiences, routine and difficult, humorous and sad, that he had over the years of practice. When he first establishes his business in California, he needs to supplement his income, and he does it by drawing cartoons about veterinarians and their patients. These are published in professional magazines and in book form; a number of them are included in his book. He cares for animals at a park that trains dolphins, sea lions, seals, and a whale. Not a great deal is known at that time about medically treating creatures of the sea, and as a result he has some unusual ordeals. Miller is also called to treat unusual animals being used in films, as well as circus animals. Once all members of a big cat act—tigers, a black panther, lions, a leopard, pumas, and a jaguar—have been fed poisoned meat; he is able to save them all. The author says he has treated many animals, but the ones he actually fears are full-grown chimpanzees. He uses one experience to explain his fear. Some people are entranced by wild animals native to this country; he tells, for example, about a skunk that two young women want descented and about a fox that has been run over by a car and is brought in by a professional writer who has found it and wants it saved.

Miller has a lively sense of humor, and his many anecdotes are entertaining. He has a deep appreciation for the out-of-doors, and his description of the beauty of a scene that has often helped relieve his extreme fatigue or tension also inspires the reader. James Herriot has written a very appreciative introduction of Miller's book and of his cartoons.

Every chapter has incidents that can be used for booktalks. Calling at the wrong house and sending the lady of the house into shock, pages 37–39; attempting to treat a mature chimpanzee, pages 66–69; solving the problem of a bull with a four-foot piece of garden hose in its stomach, pages 79–84; treating an injured fox, pages 91–94; finding a basset hound puppy for a family, pages 95–98; and taking care of the most courageous animal Miller has ever known, pages 116–18, are a few suggestions.

My young readers had read and liked some of James Herriot's books but were not interested in reading the fourth one, although it is written as well as the earlier ones. His *The Lord God Made Them All* is a bit different from his other books because he includes, besides stories about his local patients, a voyage with a load of pedigreed sheep to Russia, where he visits a school in the port city without being escorted by officials, and a flight to Istanbul with some cattle. He has a narrow escape on this trip. In *My Animal Kingdom, One by One,* David Taylor tells of being on call to zoos and wild-animal parks in England, Europe, and the Near East. His patients have ranged from killer whales to baby pandas. Some experiences are humorous, some touching, and others tragic. Although Dr. Camuti began as an animal doctor, he eventually narrowed his practice to cats, and he likes to make house calls. The experiences he describes in *All My Patients Are under the Bed* are primarily amusing, but he does include a few sad episodes. In *The Animals Come First* Mary Bowring, the wife of an English country veterinarian, describes her husband's work and some of the most interesting, most exasperating, most touching, and sometimes most amusing cases. Mary helps her husband in surgery and often makes calls with him. A different kind of story about helping animals is *Sherlock Bones* by John Keane, who tells how he got into the business of finding missing animals and describes his experiences working with people who have lost their pets. Jean Embry began her work with wild animals as a part-time attendant in the Children's Zoo in San Diego. She intended to become a veterinarian, but her work at the zoo developed into that of goodwill ambassador, including the training of animals for public appearances and television. *My Wild World* is the title of her book. In *Dr. Wildlife,* veterinarian Rory Foster becomes so interested in saving the lives of injured wild animals and birds that he and his partner build an addition on their animal hospital. *The Making of a Woman Vet* by Sally Haddock is different in that most of the story is about Sally's four years in veterinary school and her summer employment working with animals.

Moran, Richard

    Cold Sea Rising.   1986.   Arbor House.

    At 6:30 A.M. on October 15, 1995, the geologist on duty at the Geodynamics Branch of the Goddard Space Flight Center in Greenbelt, Maryland, receives a warning that there has been a monstrous magma discharge in Antarctica, directly below the Ross Ice Shelf. Dr. Melissa McCoy, glaciologist on duty at the America Antarctic Research Station at McMurdo

Sound, goes aloft to survey the area. She and the pilot discover that the Ross Ice Shelf has broken away from the coast and is moving north toward the Pacific Ocean. Melissa's father, Adm. Waldo Rankin, one of the world's foremost Antarctic scientists, is notified and takes charge. With the shelf free, the entire West Antarctic Ice Sheet could slide into the ocean. As the ice melted, the sea level would rise, inundating the great ports of the world. A giant evacuation would have to take place on islands and continents, and yet many lives would be lost. Melissa's husband, Josh McCoy, is the *New York Times*'s most respected reporter. Although he and Melissa are more or less permanently estranged, Rankin wants Josh in New Zealand where he will be immediately available when the admiral needs him to make announcements. The *New York Times* will have the responsibility of warning the world. Then a seer, a 128-year-old Maori living on Campbell Island 400 miles south of New Zealand, warns his people to take refuge in mountain caves because a great wave, twice as high as the greatest tsunami that has ever struck Campbell Island, will hit the next day at noon. Thus, a second catastrophe takes place as this wave makes its way north, hitting New Zealand's South Island, Australia, and the islands north to Japan. Having been informed by one of their satellites about the disaster building in Antarctica, the Russians decide to land troops and weapons on the ice shelf in a plan to conquer the world. However, the Japanese fishing fleet has been wiped out when it collides with the ice shelf in dense fog, and three survivors who managed to land on the shelf accidentally play an important role in foiling the Russians. Although there are major disasters, Rankin eventually finds a way to reverse the course of the shelf.

The story certainly holds the reader's attention; tension is high as the author switches from one group to another to keep the reader up-to-date on events. However, Rankin's plan to change the course of the shelf takes place without a hitch, a not-very-realistic conclusion.

For a booktalk use pages 9–14, 17–20, 30–32, which give a little more detail than the first part of the note above. This should be enough to interest readers.

Why did a Navy plane carrying 196 personnel suddenly disintegrate? Why are TVs and radios outdoors in California disintegrating and killing the listeners? This is the problem confronting Dr. Michael Zelman, special investigator for the President of the United States. The reader follows Basil Jackson's taut story, *State of Emergency*, as Zelman and his staff strive to solve the mystery. There are two well-controlled sex scenes. Any reader interested in natural disasters will want to read at least part of *The Violent Face of Nature* by Kendrick Frazier. He describes the damage done by specific tornadoes, earthquakes, floods, hurricanes, blizzards, and volcanoes. Parts of these chapters may be a bit technical for many younger readers, but they will find many interesting facts in the second section of the book—about how to prepare for a disaster, our increasing vulnerability to disasters, and responses to disaster.

Nathan, Robert

Portrait of Jennie.   1939.   Knopf.

> Where I come from
> Nobody knows
> And where I'm going
> Everything goes
> The Wind blows
> The sea flows—
> And nobody knows.

These are the words sung tunelessly in the dusk of a misty winter evening to the discouraged young painter, Eben Adams, by a small girl he has stopped to watch playing hop-scotch in the park. She is well dressed but in an old-fashioned coat, gaiters, and bonnet. After Eben has spoken to her, they walk through the park together, talking. She says that her name is Jennie Appleton and that her parents are actors playing at the Hammerstein Music Hall. With a shock Eben remembers that the theater burned down years before, when he was a boy. The little girl's hand is warm and firm in his; she is not a ghost, and he is not dreaming. When they reach the end of the park, Eben says good-bye to Jennie. "I wish you'd wait for me to grow up but you won't, I guess," she says, and in a moment she is walking away down the mall. Later, in his studio, Eben sketches a portrait of Jennie as he remembers her in her quaint clothes. Four days later he sells the sketch, and this is the beginning of his success as an artist. From time to time

Eben sees Jennie again, and always she seems to be taller and older then he remembers her. When he remarks about it, she replies that she is hurrying. The young painter's skill seems to improve, especially when he is painting Jennie, and she comes to his room occasionally to pose for him. When he takes a finished portrait to the art dealer who has befriended him, the man is so impressed with the masterpiece that he gives Eben $300 on account, hoping to sell "Jennie" to a museum or private collector. Months pass before Jennie comes again—this time to spend a whole day. She is now a young lady and is being sent to France to school for two years. Eben spends the summer on Cape Cod, and in late September in a great hurricane Jennie appears to him again, struggling futilely to escape the clutching sea. Eben tries to save her, but she is torn from his arms by the monstrous waves.

This is a strange tale, a story of mixed time sequences, with an odd air of dream and unreality that poetically evokes the poignancies of life and love moving in the irreversible stream of time. Those who like fantasies are captivated by Nathan's charming book.

Great care should be taken with this delicate story when attempting a booktalk—so much depends on the way in which it is told. A lengthy description is dangerous lest the mood be lost. The first two meetings may be used, stressing Jennie's desire to grow up fast and emphasizing the strangeness of the two occasions, pages 3–14 and 43–52.

The fantasy theme runs through several adult books that teenagers enjoy. *Green Mansions* by William H. Hudson is the love story of the beautiful birdgirl Rima and a young political refugee in a Venezuelan forest. *Seal-Woman* by Ronald Lockley is the story of Shian who, as a child, lives very close to nature and the sea. As an adult she lives with and follows many of the habits of the seals, even to the point of raising her child as a seal mother would. A very different but very appealing love story.

Owens, Mark and Delia

Cry of the Kalahari. 1984. Houghton Mifflin.

Mark and Delia, who met as graduate students at the University of Georgia, were interested in Africa, and when they heard a visiting lecturer say that more than two-thirds of Africa's wildlife had been eliminated, they both wanted to go there to study an African carnivore in its natural ecosystem. If they waited until they finished their doctorates, it might be too late, so they quit school to earn money to go to Africa. They married in 1973 and a year later took off for Africa with $600 and their few possessions in their backpacks. It takes them two months in the capital of Botswana to get research permits. Meanwhile, they do some work on a third-hand Land Rover they have bought, and eventually they take off for Maun looking for a good place to begin their research. Finally a professional hunter suggests Deception Valley. Following his directions they reach the spot in the Kalahari Desert that will be their home for the next seven years. As they look out over the fossilized riverbed, they see herds of springbok, gemsbok, and hartebeest. Where these animals feed, there will be carnivores; their plan to observe a little-known predator eliminates lions, jackals, cheetahs, and wild dogs. Sitting in the truck at night close to the animals, they notice a creature with emerald-green eyes—most have yellow ones. The animal is elusive, but eventually they discover it is a brown hyena about which little is known. When Mark and Delia first begin, they have to sleep in the truck and prepare meals beside it. Several things go wrong, their money is almost gone, and they are almost ready to give up when a man from the Botswana Department of Surveys drops in bringing them some fresh food. Two days later he is back with a tent, a folding table and chairs, some cooking equipment, and four drums of water; soon the mail brings them a grant from the National Geographic Society. They continue writing to various organizations, describing their work, and when they need more money, someone always supplies enough for them to carry on. Eventually they need a small plane to complete their work, and one is provided. Although their major study is of the hyena, they cannot overlook the lions that live close to their camp and are frequent visitors and much interested in them.

Mark and Delia are an extraordinary young couple deeply devoted to persuading the Botswana government and those who can help in other countries that the Kalahari is worth saving from mining companies and cattle ranchers. Most people could not have tolerated the conditions under which they live—close to animals that have never before seen humans; uninteresting food, often in limited amounts; primitive living conditions, even in the last years when things are 100 percent improved; remoteness from other people and supplies; constant danger; and terrible summer heat. Their close relationship with the animals is remarkable. The animals are not afraid of them and often come into the camp, and while the Owenses are wary, they are not afraid. Some of their experiences are breathtaking, many are amusing, and all are fascinating.

There are innumerable episodes for booktalks. Try Mark and Delia's first visitor in camp and the help he gives them, pages 30–35. Chapter 3 tells of their fighting a prairie fire and also of Delia waking in their small tent to see two male lions looking through the door at her. Delia tells of the creatures who share their camp, pages 89–94. On their way back from Maun one day, the meet a professional hunter and his party, and he invites them to stay overnight. They enjoy, free of charge, the sumptuous service, accommodations, and food for which the customers pay from $750 to $1,000 a day, pages 190–94. One time Delia tries to prepare a landing place for Mark and the plane in a new area, not knowing a strange pride of lions is watching her, pages 210–12. Librarians should read this book; their enthusiasm will attract readers.

Jeannette Hanby, author of *Lions Share*, takes a different approach in recording her observations of lions. She and her husband, David Bygott, lived in the Serengeti for four years, and she tries to give a lion's view of the lions' lives and people do not enter it. Bygott's beautiful drawings, not only of lions and cubs but of all the other creatures of the area, enhance most of the pages. This is a thoroughly enjoyable account. In order to get his master's degree in wildlife management, Chris McBride had to do at least six months' fieldwork. He chose as his project a pride of lions in Africa, which is his homeland. The story of his experiences, some of them hair-raising, is found in *The White Lions of Timbavati*, which is illustrated with excellent photographs. A couple of years later he wrote *Operation White Lion*, in which he tells of searching for and capturing three white cubs. Because lions hunt at night, the white lions could be easily seen and would starve to death when their mother no longer fed them; they would be better off in a zoo or animal park where they would be fed and cared for. McBride's approach to lions is quite different from that of the Owenses.

Rance, Joseph, and *Arei Hato*

Bullet Train. 1980. Morrow.

The *Hikari* 109, one of the fleet of Japanese bullet trains, covers the 729 miles from Tokyo to Hakata in six hours, fifty-six minutes. Everything about the movement of the train is handled in the Operations Room of Centralized Traffic Control under the watchful eyes of Operations Chief Hiroshi. Every bullet train is under constant surveillance. On one hot summer day, there are about fifteen hundred passengers aboard when Motorman Aoki receives clearance from the station and opens the main throttle control. When the computer ATC takes over, Aoki just sits back and watches his instrument panel. When the *Hikari* 109 is twenty-three minutes out of Tokyo, the chief of the National Railways Police receives a bomb threat. He is told that if the speed of *Hikari* 109 falls below fifty miles per hour, the bomb will automatically detonate. The caller proves it is no hoax by blowing up a freight engine with a similar device. A guard examines the luggage on the *Hikari* 109, and the assistant engineer checks the switchboards and maintenance entry points: no bomb. Suddenly in the Operations Room a duty controller announces that there has been a breakdown just seven miles ahead of *Hikari* 109. The bullet train will have to be switched to another line, but unfortunately there is already another train approaching on the track. Aoki has to slow down as much as possible but keep above fifty miles an hour. He does not think he can, but he manages to keep the speed at fifty-two miles an hour. Finally Hiroshi tells him to hold it at that speed for two more minutes, fifteen seconds, and then take it to seventy-five. These are tense moments for the reader as well as for the participants. The two trains just barely miss one another. The bomber calls demanding $5 million in American money, and the Japanese government agrees to supply it. The Japanese ask the U.S. Army 14th Ordinance Group based outside Tokyo for help, and when the man assigned to the duty is briefed at the Operations Room, he realizes that his wife is on the train. Word comes through that if the bomb is under the train, there is no way that they can reach it from inside the train. However, after anxious hours they find a way and are able to stop the train.

The suspense is well maintained, and the reader fears for the safety of the crew and passengers; at the last possible moment the bomb is defused. Some interesting characters are quite realistically depicted, both on the train and in the Operations Room. The police seem to be more interested in catching the criminals than in saving the people on the train, and at times the two groups almost work against one another.

A booktalk can just set the scene, which should be enough to arouse interest in the story.

Zed by Rosemary Harris tells of a small boy who, with his father, a favorite uncle, and the employees of an office building, is held by Arab terrorists for four days. It is a superior story of high suspense, and the young people who hold their breath over it could be introduced to *Bullet Train. Maxwell's Train* by Christopher Hyde is the taut tale of a ruthless gang of European terrorists who hijack an Amtrak train in Washington, D.C., that is carrying $35 million in cash to Boston. Their preparation for the crime is so thorough and the takeover so violent that the passengers are helpless, but as the train proceeds toward Canada, a variety of people begin to make plans to retake the train.

Retton, Mary Lou, and *Karolyi, Bela* with *John Powers*

Mary Lou: Creating an Olympic Champion.   1986.
McGraw-Hill.

The youngest of five children, Mary Lou Retton grows up in the coal-mining town of Fairmont, West Virginia. Her father has been an athlete, and all the children are into sports. Mary Lou becomes interested in gymnastics, and when she is seven, classes are begun in town. Soon she makes up her mind that she will be in the 1984 Olympics. At twelve she goes to the Class I Nationals in Tulsa and makes a good showing. She realizes that she needs better training than that available at home. She has seen some of Bela Karolyi's students perform, and so she talks with her parents about the possibility of working with him. At a meet in Reno, her Dad talks with Karolyi, who finds a family with which Mary Lou can live in Houston. It is a difficult decision for her parents to make, and it is difficult for

Mary Lou to leave her family at age fourteen. Her parents drive her down to Texas and settle her in her new home and school. The rest of the account tells of her training, coaches, competitions, and triumphs. Karolyi's story alternates with hers. He and his wife Martha are Romanians; they operate a school for gymnasts in a coal-mining town in Transylvania. Their training methods are different because their pupils start working at a very early age. By the time they can enter competition, they are really experts. They beat Russia's best, who are grown women, and Russia does not approve. The Soviets make life so difficult for the Karolyis that they defect on a trip with a team to the United States. They have to sacrifice all their possessions at home and begin life here with no money and with no knowledge of English. They rapidly learn to speak English and take any kind of work available until they meet people interested in founding a school of gymnastics. The United States has never shone in international gymnastics competition, and the idea of possible success grows as Karolyi's students begin to appear in meets. This is the story of the Karolyis' success as trainers also.

Mary Lou tells her own story with teenage enthusiasm; Bela tells his in fractured English, and readers feel as if they are actually listening to both people speak. There are photographs of Mary Lou on the vault, on the beam, on the floor and the bars, but unless readers know something about gymnastics, they may not realize just what the performer is doing.

There really are no episodes for a booktalk, but in chapters 3 and 7 Mary Lou tells of making the decision to leave Fairmont and of her first days working with Karolyi in Houston. There are enough facts there to establish some empathy between the reader and the performing teenagers.

Chris Evert Lloyd frankly discusses her career in tennis in *Chrissie: My Own Story.* She includes training, playing, dating, friendships, pranks, and marriage to John Lloyd. In *Winning Women* Paul Wade tells how quickly women athletes have been catching up to men in many sports in the last ten years. Because they have a better sense of balance, greater stamina, and more flexibility, they are surpassing men in some categories. Wade says very little about individuals, but Tony Duffy's excellent action photographs tell a great deal. In *Basketball My Way* Nancy Lieberman concentrates on technique rather than her growing-up years and her basketball experiences. Once the youngest member of a winning Olympic team, she now plays with a professional basketball team; her book is for those who want to improve their play. In *Passing Shots: Pam Shriver on Tour*, Pamela comments candidly and briefly on her play, male and female friends, competition, tournaments, and family.

Rowe, Jack

Brandywine. 1984. Watts.

Maggie and Patrick Gallagher and their three boys consider themselves fortunate to have been able to leave Ireland and find work in the United States in 1800. Another Irish family, the Feeneys, settle nearby. After a short time both men go to work for Irenee du Pont, who is building powder mills along the Brandywine not far from Wilmington, Delaware. Patrick, a skilled stonemason, supervises the cutting and setting of stone for the mills. In 1810 strained relations between England and the United States cause an increased demand for gunpowder. The Gallaghers' oldest son, Brendan, has been hired to drive a team delivering orders for powder. He and Noreen Feeney have fallen in love and make plans to leave the area so that he can start his own freight line, but their plans do not materialize. When they marry, they move in with Brendan's parents. Fortunately Maggie and Noreen get along very well. Brendan is gone for weeks at a time, and Noreen is disturbed and unhappy. In bed her husband is inexperienced and not considerate of her feelings and needs. When she visits her sister, a maid in the du Pont home, she meets, by accident, Louis Jardinere, a French aristocrat, and Noreen's beauty fires his lust. Unfortunately he seduces her, and she willingly submits because he is an accomplished lover. However, she soon comes to her senses and breaks off the relationship. With the powder business growing, du Pont chooses Brendan to oversee the whole freight business. With Brendan home all the time, he and Noreen are able to establish a new relationship and are happy. She soon knows she is pregnant. Shortly before the baby is born, there is a terrible explosion at the mill, and half the workers die. The Gallaghers lose their twin sons, and the Feeneys lose their oldest boy. That night Noreen's baby is born, and she knows as soon as she sees her daughter that Brendan is not the father. As the years pass, the Underground Railroad grows, and a station is set up near the du Pont mills. The last part of the story concerns the arrival of a group of slaves from Virginia. The way these various problems are worked out is satisfying, and the story ends happily.

Rowe's ancestors were among the early workers at the du Pont mills, and he knows the locality and the people. His main characters are well developed and become people the reader admires and would like to meet. There is plenty of action to keep the story moving.

Pages 16–28 introduce Maggie, Patrick, and Mr. du Pont; set the scene for the story; and tell how Patrick became du Pont's stonemason. Or the booktalker may prefer the information about a neighbor's plan to ruin the new mill unless du Pont pays him an exorbitant price for a useless plot of ground on the Brandywine above the new mill; du Pont and his men foil that plan, pages 44–69.

Another intriguing story about immigrant families in America, *Susquehanna* by Harriet Segal, begins in 1877 when Isaac and Aaron Hillman, Jews from Russia, bring their families to America and settle in Pennsylvania. This book, which ends in 1962, follows three generations. In *Gates of Grace°* by Evelina Chao, young Mei-yu and Kung-chiao escape from the Communists in China and come to Chinatown in New York City, where a relative gives them an allowance to enable Kung-chiao to finish his education. The young husband is murdered just after he graduates, and Mei-yu is left to support their daughter. An aristocratic old Chinese woman helps her and engineers another marriage. The University of Nebraska has recently brought out a new edition of Bess Streeter Aldrich's lovely story of early Nebraska, *Spring Came on Forever.* It begins with the love story of Matthias Meier and Amalia Stoltz, a German immigrant's daughter. Amalia is forced to agree to marry her father's old friend, and the couple go to live on a farm in Nebraska. Matthias follows her but arrives too late to prevent the marriage. He settles in what becomes the state capital and goes into business. Although they never meet again, fate brings two of their great-grandchildren together as husband and wife.

Schnell, Jonathan

The Fate of the Earth. 1982. Knopf.

Jonathan Schnell is very much concerned about the situation in which nations have placed themselves by building nuclear weapons. To impress the reader with the seriousness of the matter, he begins by describing a full-scale holocaust and its results—the destruction of all life and the death of the earth. He discusses the many ways in which a person could die in a holocaust. He names three events that might lead to a nuclear attack. These include an accidental triggering, eruptions between smaller nations that might draw in the superpowers, and an international crisis in which fear that the enemy might use nuclear weapons prompts the first use. Schnell explains why no one could survive a holocaust and describes the experience of people at Hiroshima, which endured only one small bomb. What happened in Japan was less than a millionth part of a holocaust at present levels of nuclear armament. He states that if the nations of the Northern Hemisphere were destroyed, the oceans could be poisoned, the climate could be changed by damage to the ozone layer, and ultraviolet radiation could cause blindness in humans and animals. As a result the Southern Hemisphere could also be affected. There is no evidence that any species, once extinguished, has ever evolved again. So if human life were extinguished on earth, there would be no future generations. Schnell outlines three principles of life that should be found in a new common world from which nuclear weapons have been eliminated: respect for human life, respect for the earth, and respect for God or nature. He claims that we are living on borrowed time; only the complete elimination of nuclear weapons can save us.

None of my readers wanted to tackle this book, but librarians across the country voted to include this important work. Only the very best readers may be able to get through the entire book, but the first and last sections can be read and understood by average readers.

A librarian who wants to use this book for a booktalk could quote pages 17–26, which describe what happens when a nuclear device is dropped on a city.

The Cold and the Dark: The World after Nuclear War is a report of talks and questions and answers heard in 1984 at the

Conference on the Long-Term Worldwide Biological Consequences of Nuclear War. Outstanding scientists spoke from the platform and others were in the audience to ask questions or were panel members. Peter Wyden's *Day One: Before Hiroshima and After* takes the reader from the conception of the bomb to its realization, the decision to use it, and the aftermath. See Sidney Lanier on page 96 for fiction about nuclear holocausts.

Severin, Tim

The Sinbad Voyage. 1983. Putnam.

Having read stories about Sinbad's many adventures in his seven voyages to the Far East, Severin wants to know just how many of the man's experiences are based on the real achievements of Arabian sailors. In 1980 Tim, starting from Oman on the Arabian peninsula, sails across the Seven Seas to China in an Omani sailing ship that is sewed together with four hundred miles of coconut fiber. It takes about five years to construct the ship and to make the six thousand–mile voyage. Fortunately the Sultan of Oman becomes interested in Severin's idea and volunteers to finance it. Severin selects the trees (aini) in India for the ship's timbers. Another type of tree (poon) has to be found for the spars and mast. In order for the vessel to survive the possible storms on the voyage, the coconut rope used in the sewing has to be specially prepared and hand twisted. On New Year's Day, 1980, the work platform on which the ship would be built is ready; the work has to be completed by November 18, 1980. The author has carefully selected his workers and supervises them skillfully. The rope workers come from the Laccadives, islands off the coast of India; the shipwrights who prepare the ship's mainframes with hand tools are Arabian. The men like Severin and work long hours. They obviously enjoy themselves, usually singing lively work songs, and they have prodigious appetites, relishing their two breakfasts, lunch, and supper. At day's end they are too exhausted to do anything but tumble into bed. It doesn't seem possible that the ship can be finished in time, but it is. The sultan names the ship *Sohar* in honor of the ancient port city of Oman. Meanwhile the crew has been hired, and several oceanographers who sign on for parts of the voyage also have to serve as crew. They have many adventures with squalls, fickle winds and currents, torrential rains, sharks, and shoals. The voyage is considered a great success, and the vessel is shipped back to Oman to become a monument to the country's seafaring history.

The author does not bore the reader with too much detail but still makes one feel a part of the project from the beginning to the end. There are many colorful characters who furnish touches of humor. One learns painlessly many interesting facts about the customs of the people in the Far East. The total devotion to duty of the crew's eight Omani sailors is beautiful. Other crew members learn from them and are efficient under normal conditions, but stormy weather demands the total competence of the Omani, who get very little rest at times.

Many splendid color photographs of the ship and the crew and their activities are included, as well as reproductions of illustrations from *The Arabian Nights' Entertainments*, translated by Edward William Lane. Maps on the endpapers trace the *Sohar*'s route.

There are a number of incidents suitable for booktalks. For example, a worker receives a telegram from home saying that a daughter has died, and the man asks for time off to go home. Severin suspects chicanery because the men have just been paid. They would have enjoyed a little vacation if Tim had not foiled their plan, pages 65–67. When the ship is in port in India, one of the men asks for Severin's permission to marry a local girl. The incident involves a custom strange to us, pages 129–32. When Severin has selected the spot on the beach for the platform on which they will build the ship, he finds a hut there that belongs to two mechanics who repair boat engines. They promise to move it but do not. Tim finds a way to solve that problem, pages 51–53.

Thor Heyerdahl's books can be suggested as follow-up titles. In *Brendan Voyage* Severin describes sailing from Ireland to Newfoundland with three companions in a leather boat that he designed. The story of Jason and the golden fleece is familiar to many young readers. In *The Jason Voyage*, Severin and his crew sail and row an open boat similar to Jason's from Greece to Georgia in the Soviet Union on the Black Sea.

Tracking Marco Polo.   1986.   Peter Bedrick.

When Tim was in prep school, he had been entranced with Marco Polo's journey from Venice to China and back. In 1961 he is studying geography at Oxford, and Marco Polo's book is used as a reference. This ignites Tim's interest again, and he decides to spend his next summer vacation following Marco Polo's route. He finds two other young men, Stan and Mike, who are also interested in the adventure. They decide to use two motorcycles with sidecars for transportation, even though they know little about the vehicles. They wear black uniforms with light blue helmets and tall black jackboots—an impressive attire, especially among foreign peoples. They go by way of Venice, which had been Marco Polo's home and starting point. Then they cross Yugoslavia and Bulgaria. It isn't until they reach Istanbul that they feel they are really seeing things as the Venetians had seen them. They find that the modern road generally follows the Old Silk Road that the caravan traveled. As they move along, they read about what Marco Polo had seen. If they reach a village and can't readily see what he described, they search until they find it. For example, they want to see the beautiful carpets made in Bunyan, but the village is a collection of mud houses with no sign whatsoever of carpet making. They persist in asking questions and finally learn that almost every house has a heavy wooden loom on which a lovely carpet is being woven. There are similar incidents with Ehram in Erzinjan, the silk fabric in Yezd, the mineral water baths on the road to Erzurum, and the Apples of Paradise on the road to Hormuz. Almost everywhere they find the people friendly, and although many are desperately poor, they often share their simple food or a cup of hot tea. Mike and Tim have some hair-raising adventures in the Valley of the Assassins, and Tim breaks a bone in his foot. Thereafter he travels by bus with one leg in a cast while Mike and Stan take a different route to Kabul in Afghanistan by motorcycle. From there they have to return to England because classes are to begin in three weeks.

The account was written shortly after their return to England and published there in 1964. Since then Severin has made a name for himself by writing about voyages he has made, following the paths of early explorers in the types of vessels they used. This book, for which he has written a new foreword, has now been published in the United States. A map accompanies each section of their travels showing how closely they paralleled Marco Polo's route. The story has plenty of action and suspense and is fun to read.

For a booktalk, use pages 2–4, 10–11, 40–47, telling how Stan, Mike, and Tim get together and about their stay in Istanbul.

Tim quotes often from Marco Polo's own book, and some readers will want to read it. Henry H. Hart is a scholar who has studied many sources for accounts of Marco Polo's adventures. His book, *Marco Polo, Venetian Adventurer,* is remarkably readable (even the many footnotes), although it honestly doesn't look it. It will probably be of interest only to the young person seriously interested in travel through forbidding territory in the thirteenth century. *The Travels of Marco Polo,* a beautiful book by Cottie A. Burland, will give young people a very pleasant way to follow the famous Venetian on his journey. Part of the text is in the words of the author, and part is in Marco Polo's words translated into English. The Czech photographer Werner Forman followed Marco Polo's route and took lovely photographs along the way. Even if junior high readers are not interested in Robin Hanbury-Tenison's struggles to save the Indians of Brazil and the natives in the interior of Indonesia from their governments' ruthlessness, they will like his trip by jeep from Recife on the coast of Brazil across the mostly roadless continent to Lima, Peru. He also travels from the coast of Venezuela in a rubber boat south to Buenos Aires. Later in a Hovercraft he goes from Dakar in Senegal along several rivers to the interior of Africa. He describes his adventures in *Worlds Apart.*

Simpson, Dorothy

Dead on Arrival. 1986. Scribner.

Detective Inspector Luke Thanet receives a phone call at home late one cold, wet November evening telling him of a murder and calling him back to duty. Steve Long, a young man who lives in an old mansion that has been converted into small apartments, has been killed; he was hit on the back of his head by a blunt instrument as he sat on a davenport with his back to the door behind him. There are a number of other tenants to be interviewed as well as relatives who live in the area. One of these is Steve's identical twin, Geoffrey, who has been raised by his mother's sister and her husband. Only Geoffrey is on somewhat friendly terms with Steve, who is considered obnoxious by his half-brothers and their wives. In fact, Steve's wife has left him because of his disposition. Several of those interviewed might well be the murderer, but Thanet is not ready to accuse anyone without further investigation. Chief Inspector Hines is also working on a case that might turn out to be murder. A grey jacket with a red dragon's head on the back is involved, and the police ask the public over television to report anyone wearing one. When a man comes into the police station, Thanet interviews him because Hines is absent. He learns that the boy living across the street from the man has worn such a jacket. Shortly after this Thanet discovers that Geoffrey gave Steve a jacket on their birthday but was unable to celebrate with him because he had a date with a new girlfriend. Bitterly disappointed, Steve apparently went out and picked up a girl at a pub. Her death is the one Hines is investigating. Pondering the facts of the case, in the middle of the night, Thanet has a bright idea and the next day does some checking. Geoffrey is in the process of moving, but he welcomes Thanet. It is then that the reader learns that Geoffrey is dead and Steve has assumed Geoffrey's role, but Steve claims he did not murder his brother, and this proves to be true.

As usual Dorothy Simpson has presented a well-plotted mystery in which Thanet has to do a lot of digging for facts before the case is solved. The author rounds out her story with incidents from Thanet's home life, thus making him more real and likable.

A booktalk can be built from the first two chapters, which give Thanet's first knowledge about Steve's death and his visit with the landlady who lived below Steve.

In *The Night She Died* a young married woman is found dead just inside the front door by her husband when he returns from night school. Careful questioning and observation by Thanet turn up several suspects, and he eventually solves the mystery. In *Puppet for a Corpse* by Simpson, a prominent physician has apparently committed suicide. Thanet takes over the case and unearths enough information to prove that the doctor had attempted to frame someone for his murder. In *Six Feet Under,* also by Simpson, Thanet finds three neighbors of a murdered woman reluctant to talk, and much of what he does learn seems irrelevant. But patience and careful questioning finally give him enough information to determine who the murderer is. Another mystery that appeals to young people is *A Six Letter Word for Death* by Patricia Moyers, in which Henry Tibbett, chief superintendent of the Crime Division of Scotland Yard, solves a murder. Shortly before Tibbett is to be guest speaker at a meeting of the Guess Who Club, a group of mystery-story authors who write under pen names, he begins to receive a portion of a crossword puzzle every few days. The puzzle hints at murder for gain on the part of several people whose names appear in the puzzle. What is supposed to be a joke at Tibbett's expense turns out to be murder, tragedy, and disgrace for several of Tibbett's audience. In *Rest in Pieces* by Ralph McInerny, Father Dowling is asked to help the son of the ruling family of Costa Verde, a Latin American country, to en-roll under an assumed name in an American university where he will be safe from assassins. The seemingly simple request turns out to be quite the opposite.

Thompson, Estelle

Hunter in the Dark. 1978. Walker.

Two years before the story begins, Philip Blair had been attacked by three young men on a busy city street. As a result he was permanently blind, and so he broke his engagement to Penny Cosgrove. But he kept his apartment because it was fa-miliar and not far from the bus that went past the boys' school where he taught. When he hears someone near him one morn-ing at the bus stop, he asks the person to tell him when his bus comes. The voice that answers belongs to a girl probably ten or twelve. As they stand there talking, a car draws up, and a man's voice says, "Hello, Linda. Hop in—I'm passing the school." The child gets into the car. That night as he listens to the news, Philip hears that the body of a twelve-year-old girl who lived in his neighborhood has been found in a deserted area. A wait-ress in the milk bar across from the bus stop has described Philip to the police, and they ask that he contact them. Philip calls immediately but acknowledges he can be of little help because of his blindness. A few days later he stops in the milk bar and talks with the waitress. She states that another twelve-year-old girl wearing the same uniform had drowned two weeks earlier. The police have said there was no foul play in that case. The next day Philip calls a friend, Des Maddock, who works in the traffic division and asks him if the police still think the first girl's death was an accident, and Des confirms. Shortly, the waitress calls Philip to ask if he thinks she can get a reward if she gives some more information in the case. He thinks not. The next morning's newscast tells of the waitress's accidental death. Philip calls the police to tell them of the woman's conversation with him. Once more Philip confers with Des, and a few days later Penny comes to see him! Des thinks Philip needs a pair of eyes if he is going to carry on a private inquiry into the deaths. The author does not give the villain away but keeps the reader informed of Philip and Penny's progress. Events happen so fast in the last few pages that the readers will hold their breath.

The story is unusual in that a blind man solves a crime, and this intrigued my readers very much. The plot is well thought out, and the ending is a surprise.

Philip's meeting with Linda at the bus stop and the report of her murder should be sufficient to arouse interest in reading the book, pages 5–10, 14.

Also suggest *Hidden Wrath,* by Stella Phillipos, which takes place near Meddenham. Detective Inspector Furnival is the chief investigator of what could be an accidental death or the murder of a librarian who, with several helpers, had been cataloging an old collection of books at Braseley Hall, an adult college. In *The Case of the Poisoned Eclairs* by E. V. Cunningham, Masao Masuto, a brilliant Nisei detective on the Beverly Hills police force, is put on a poison case. Four women, considering the calories involved, refuse to eat eclairs at a bridge party, and the maid to whom the food is given dies of botulism. In *The Case of the Sliding Pool,* also by Cunningham, Masao Masuto is given a week to solve a thirty-year-old murder. A skeleton is found in the rock under a swimming pool that, loosened by weeks of rain, slides down a hillside. The outcome surprises even Masuto. The young readers were especially enthusiastic about Cunningham's stories. In *The Poisoned Web* by Anna

Clark, two unmarried Oxford students living in the attic apartment of a house belonging to the widow of a well-liked professor are unknowingly drawn into the malicious old lady's plot to cause her hated daughter harm in one way or another.

Thorne, Victoria

Longsword. 1982. St. Martin's.

Sir Gervase Escot of War is his uncle's heir and has managed his uncle's estate for some time. Suddenly the old man decides to marry an attractive young widow, and in a short time Gervase is accused of theft, tried, and convicted. He manages to escape and is making his way to the coast to take a ship abroad when he comes upon Castle Malling. There are several beggars at the castle gates, and when they attack the lady dispensing welfare, Gervase rescues her. As a result he is invited to spend the night but declines until she says he can have a bed in the infirmary. He leaves the next morning and later contracts smallpox. When he comes to Malling again, he is dressed in rags and can barely walk. He is sure no one will recognize him, but the lady does and takes him in. One day the old man in the next room suddenly calls out for help, but no one comes; he has upset his candle; his bedding has caught fire; and he is too infirm to get out of bed. Though Gervase is so weak he can barely walk, he manages to snatch off the bedding. Hamo, the old man, has been for many years the steward of the estates of Malling, and when the two men become friendly, Hamo learns that Gervase can read and write. He decides that Gervase should help him and later suggests Gervase should succeed him as steward. The young woman who befriended Gervase is the twin sister of Elaine, the girl to whom Gervase had been betrothed before his disgrace. Though Elaine is beautiful, she is shallow, selfish, and ignorant, while her sister, Beata, who is dark and attractive and dedicated to helping others, was promised to the church when a baby. Now Gervase has fallen in love with her and she with him, but there is no possibility of marriage. Lord Henry, owner of Malling, has planned a tournament to celebrate Christmas and Elaine's marriage to Sir Bertrand de Bors. Lord Henry orders Gervase placed in a cage, a torture chamber in the depths of the cellars. When her brother Crispin informs her of Gervase's imprisonment, Beata tells Crispin she will do a big favor for him if he will get Gervase out of the cage and hear his story. He does, and when Crispin dies as a result of injuries in the tournament, Gervase takes the place of the man who is to avenge Crispin's death. He defeats his opponent but refuses to kill him. After this, Gervase is able to clear his name and assume his title as Lord Escot.

This is an interesting and involved picture of what life was like on the estate of a wealthy noble in medieval England. Several of the characters are well drawn, and the story holds the reader's interest. Some of my group liked it very much.

After introducing Gervase, Beata, and Hamo, the booktalker can use chapter 3, in which Gervase and Beata exchange information about themselves. Also see pages 49–56.

The Lady of Rhuddesmere by Victoria Strauss depicts what seem to be two typical households during the Middle Ages, but one of these turns out to include worshippers of evil. A young reader of this story can be introduced to Longsword, which has a more pleasant ending. In *The Wind from Hastings* Morgan Llywelyn tells the story of Edyth, oldest child of Aelfgar, Earl of East Anglia. Outlawed by Edward, King of England, Aelfgar gives Edyth in marriage to Prince Griffith of Wales in return for his help against Edward. The author explicitly, but with a certain amount of delicacy, describes Edyth's introduction to a man's body on their wedding night. The reader gains respect for the prince because of his sensitivity to the virginity and innocence of his bride.

Trew, Antony

Bannister's Chart. 1984. St. Martin's.

The *Sunglow*, an aged freighter, calls at islands in the Indian Ocean along the East African coast delivering and loading mail and cargo. It has been remodeled to accommodate twenty passengers, and the brochure says it is not a floating hotel but offers an adventure cruise on a working vessel. Captain Cassidy is a middle-aged Irishman, an excellent seaman, and very likable. The crew speaks Bengali, Swahili, or Seychellois, and most of them speak some English as well. Only the first mate, Luigi Scallati, is new on the ship, and he and Cassidy do not like one another. Ali Patel, son of *Sunglow*'s owner, has promised Scallati a large reward to wreck the ship on a reef so that he can collect the insurance. One passenger on the September 24 sailing is Mrs. Beryl Clutterbutt, whose great-grandfather was shipwrecked in 1881 in the area of the cruise and spent five weeks on an uninhabited island before being rescued. The island is not on any chart, but he had made a drawing of it, and Mrs. C., as she prefers to be called, thinks there are gold ingots buried there. She enlists Cassidy's help in finding the island. On the way to their first port of call, the ship encounters a cyclone, most unusual in September, and it is a frightening experience. In getting back to its original course, the ship picks up two crew members from a Liberian bulk carrier sunk by the storm. Both are expected to work out their passage. One is unwilling and is soon recruited by Scallati to help in his plan. The activities, announced each day, consist of side trips by skimmers to interesting atolls, a barbecue on the beach of an uninhabited island, swimming off beautiful beaches, goggling at sea life in crystal-clear lagoons, and exploring coral reefs. A murder at one beach party, a passenger lost overboard at night, and the search for the treasure island add plenty of action in addition to the cyclone.

There are some well-drawn characters and plenty of mystery and excitement to hold the reader's interest. The book seems to call for a sequel and more information about the future of several of the interesting participants.

In a booktalk, after introducing Captain Cassidy, tell of the letter he received from Mrs. C. and of their first meetings, pages 16–18, 21–27, 28–41. If the speaker feels the need, the storm warning can be added, pages 67–71.

In *Running Wild* by Trew, two anti-apartheid college students in South Africa, Pippa and Andre, are tricked into helping an older dissident escape from the country. Andre's father allows him to use the family ketch and sends his older son Jan along because he is a better seaman. This is a fast-paced story of almost unbelievable events that ends happily for the young people.

Verne, Jules

Twenty Thousand Leagues under the Sea.   [1870].

Beginning in 1866, the seamen of the world have been

mystified by their contacts with a strange object or creature that is long, cigar-shaped, sometimes phosphorescent, and much larger and faster than a whale. After an alarming number of casualties and shipwrecks have been attributed to the monster, the public demands that it be destroyed, and the American frigate *Abraham Lincoln* is outfitted to track it down. M. Pierre Aronnax, a French scientist who has been doing research in Nebraska, is invited to accompany the expedition. For some time the search for the phenomenon is unsuccessful, but when the crew is about ready to give up, it comes into view. The ship gives chase, but it is late that night before it can approach close enough for Ned Land, an expert harpooner, to use his weapon. In the violent shock that follows, Professor Arannaz is thrown overboard. His drowning is prevented by his servant Conseil, who follows him into the water. The ship, damaged and out of control, drifts away from them. After several hours in the water they make contact with Ned, who has also fallen overboard but managed to climb aboard the enemy. He has discovered that it is not a narwhal but a submarine. In the morning the survivors are taken inside, where they soon meet Captain Nemo, who informs them that they are prisoners for life. He promises the professor that he will visit the land of marvels and see many wonderful sights. The prisoners find that the submarine manufactures its own electricity and has quantities of oxygen that enable it to remain submerged and its crew to walk about on the ocean floor. All the food aboard has been harvested from the sea. In the Pacific they explore the submarine forest of the island of Crespo and have several other extraordinary experiences. They enter the Mediterranean by way of a tunnel under the Isthmus of Suez and later visit lost Atlantis. Eventually they are caught in the maelstrom off the coast of Norway. It is during this last adventure that they escape and return to tell the story of their wondrous captivity.

Jules Verne had an extremely vivid imagination coupled with a rare scientific knowledge, and thus his book is fascinating to many young readers, who enjoy seeing how many of his "brain children" have become realities. This book may be used as straight adventure, as science fiction, or as an underseas story.

For a booktalk the description in chapter 10 of the inside of the submarine is of interest. The hunt in the underseas forest in chapter 16; the pearl fishery in part 2, chapter 3; and the battle with the cuttlefish, part 2, chapter 18, can also be used.

Follow the reading of this adventure tale with *The Mysterious Island*, in which four Northern men, a boy, and a dog escape in a balloon from Richmond, Virginia, during the Civil War. Driven by a terrible wind, they land on an apparently uninhabited island in the Pacific without supplies of any kind. Survival demands all their resourcefulness. Readers will also learn of Captain Nemo's fate. *The Silent World**, *The Living Sea,* and others by Cousteau tell of undersea exploration, discovery, and observation. *Around the World Submerged* by Edward L. Beach is an account of the voyage of a nuclear submarine owned by the U.S. Navy. *The Deep Range* by Arthur C. Clarke is science fiction set in the twenty-first century, when well-regulated scientific farming provides plants and animals from the oceans to feed the world's population. *A Matter of Risk* by Roy Varner and Wayne Collier is the story of the Hughes *Glomar Explorer,* the huge ship built to salvage a Russian submarine that sank north of Hawaii. It describes the ship's construction, the training of the crews, and the salvage operation.

Webster, Elizabeth

Bracken. 1984. St. Martin's.

When Jake Farrant, a famous English broadcaster, receives the verdict from his doctor that he has only a few months to live, he decides to get away by himself to some place quiet and peaceful. Luckily, a colleague, Bill Franklyn, offers him the use of his sister's cottage in the Cotswolds. Jake does not tell anyone the reason for his leaving London, but Bill manages to worm a hint from Jake's doctor by skillful questioning. When Jake reaches the cottage, the first person he meets is a friendly brown boy who offers to get milk and eggs for him. The boy also offers to show Jake a coot's nest the next day, and somehow that appeals to the man. He learns that the boy's name is Bracken and that he is a member of a gypsy band camping on a nearby farm. The youngster seems to sense that Jake is not well. He comes each day with a new suggestion of something to see or do. Bracken's enthusiasm and joy in nature are infectious. It is spring; the countryside is beautiful. Jake, who has never had time to relax and enjoy the out-of-doors, relishes his every moment with the boy. He learns that Bracken has a way with wildlife and is known in the area for being able to heal sick and injured creatures. One day he brings a young kestrel that has been winged with lead shot, and Jake holds the bird while Bracken administers to it. The boy fixes a case for the bird in Jake's yard so the man can help take care of it. Later there is a baby badger that lives there after the kestrel is able to fly away. When Bracken realizes that Jake is growing weaker, he sometimes brings two ponies, and he and Jake ride instead of walking when they explore at greater distances. Bill and Manny, another friend, come to visit and bring Jake's two grown children. Jake has never been close to them because he has been abroad a great deal and his wife has divorced him. This contact is pleasant and adds to Jake's peace of mind. The end comes quietly when Jake, one night alone, gives all he has to save a trapped bird.

This is an unusually well-written story. The lyric descriptions of Jake and Bracken's explorations are enthralling. The author gives the reader superb insight into the characters of Jake and Bracken. Although Jake has little to do with the villagers, they take him into their hearts and could not be more thoughtful and considerate. My young people liked the book.

In a booktalk introduce Jake and Bracken and then tell how Bracken saves most of the badgers that the farmers have planned to destroy and how Jake saves Bracken when the boy falls into the quarry with two badger cubs, pages 113–26.

The 79 Squares by Malcolm J. Bosse is an unusual, well-written account of the friendship between a very old man and a twelve-year-old boy who is something of a rebel. *Goodnight, Mr. Tom* by Michelle Majorian is about an abused boy evacuated from London during World War II to a small English village and his friendship with an older man. If young readers have enjoyed these two juvenile titles, they should be introduced to *Bracken. The Old Man and the Boy* by Robert Ruark tells of his companionship with his grandfather who likes to hunt and fish. The old man not only helps the boy develop his skills but also teaches him a lot about the best way to live. *Tony: Our Journey Together* by Carolyn Koons is different from the books above because a woman is the main influence on a boy.

Tony had been put in a Mexican prison when he was only five and was adopted by the author when he was eleven, coming to live with her in California. Their problems were many and very difficult, but eventually they worked them out through their reliance on God and their love for one another. In *To Fly a Kite* by Elizabeth Webster, Ellie Foster, an eighteen-year-old orphan, is drawn to Ross Mallory's garden by the lovely music she hears. Ross had been a concert pianist before a stroke crippled him. With Ellie's encouragement he begins to make a comeback. There is a rocky road ahead for both before the story ends happily.

Wells, H. G.

The War of the Worlds. [1898].

Early in the twentieth century, astronomers in England and France observe a series of ten explosions on Mars taking place regularly every twenty-four hours. Actually these turn out to be missiles that have been fired at the earth. The first lands a short distance from the storyteller's home and is, at first, thought to be a meteorite. But as it cools, the circular top of the cylinder begins to rotate, and shortly the lid falls off. Curious watchers expect a manlike creature to emerge, but when the Martians do appear, each looks more like an octopus. These beings keep the observers at a distance by using a heat ray that incinerates whatever it touches. In the pit made by the impact of the cylinder, the Martians put together their war machines. The narrator likens these to milking stools that tower over the houses and move with monstrous strides, smashing whatever they hit. They are equipped with two death-dealing weapons, the heat ray and poisonous gas. Although the British Army puts up some resistance, there is little it can do against such formidable enemies. Every twenty-four hours another cylinder lands, and more war machines are put together. As the Martians move toward London, the people flee in terror, as well they might. The witness tells of the destruction of the villages in his vicinity and of the death of many people. He also relates the experiences of his brother in London, who escapes to the Continent. At one time the narrator is in the house when a cylinder crashes into the area next door, and for twelve days he has a grandstand view of the activities of the Martians. In the end it is not man who subdues the invaders but a bacterium common to earth.

The story has great appeal for good readers from the sixth grade up. It is so realistic that one can easily believe that it actually happened.

Use the appearance of the first cylinder and the early activity of the Martians, chapters 2 and 3, for a booktalk.

Out of the Silent Planet by C. S. Lewis gives quite a different picture of the Martians, but in this instance humans from earth are visiting Mars. *The First Men in the Moon* by H. G. Wells is the story of two men who land on the moon shortly before the end of a lunar winter. With the coming of sunshine, they discover that the creatures of the moon live inside that heavenly body. One man escapes and returns to earth with little knowledge of the moon, but the other learns to communicate with the Selenites and sends back much information for a time. *Millenium* by Ben Bova depicts life on the moon and the warlike tendencies of the major powers on earth. In Arthur C. Clarke's *Imperial Earth*, a young man, who is a citizen and official of Titan, one of Saturn's moons, is invited to Earth to address Congress at the Quincentennial Program. He takes the opportunity to see something of Earth and to have a son cloned. If a young person asks if there are books about invaders from space today, suggest *Uninvited Visitors* in which Ivan Sanderson discusses UFOs from every angle. Another story of activity and possible war between other worlds and earth may be found in *Way Station* by Clifford Simak. Enoch Wallace, who looks 30 but is actually 124 years of age, is suspected of some kind of unlawful activity by two branches of U.S. Intelligence. Actually he is keeper of a house used by inhabitants of the galaxy as they travel about the universe. Enoch has a hand in solving the problems and maintaining peace.

Wharton, William

A Midnight Clear. 1982. Knopf.

The narrator of this World War II novel is William Knott, nicknamed Wont, a nineteen-year-old member of an intelligence-and-reconnaisance squad. Of the twelve members of his squad, six had been killed outside Saarbrücken when they were mistakenly sent into combat. As his story begins, it is

December, and the division has moved into the Ardennes Forest to rest and await replacements. Knott is made sergeant of the remaining men and ordered to establish an observation post between German and American lines in a chateau in the middle of the forest. On the way one of the men shoots at a German soldier partially concealed behind a tree; he falls, and when they sneak up on him, they find he has been dead for some time and propped against the tree. Later they find two dead soldiers propped together as if they are waltzing: one is an American; the other, a German. The men wonder what can be going on. When they reach the chateau, which looks like something from a French fairy tale, it is unoccupied and unfurnished. They set up guard posts uphill and downhill from the chateau and work out a schedule for duty. One night the men on guard duty hear what might be a wolf or a bad imitation of an Indian imitating a wolf. Then they hear, "Heh, ami!" They realize that a small group of German soldiers is nearby when Knott, on guard duty at the lower post, hears laughing and talking and sees a German soldier by the bridge with his rifle pointed at him. Knott lobs a grenade, but the soldier remains. Shouting and a bombardment of snowballs follow. After the Germans leave the area, the Americans discover that the German by the bridge is a snowman in uniform. Eventually the two groups of soldiers get together. One American, who speaks Yiddish, partially understands German. Sick of war, the Germans want to surrender and a plan to capture them is worked out. Vance Wilkens does not know about the scheme and is left at the chateau. When he hears the sounds of the mock battle, he runs from the chateau and fires on the Germans. All the Germans die, and the Americans lose two of their six men—a sad and ironic ending for a carefully worked-out surrender.

This unusual war story is well written and gives intimate portraits of several young American soldiers who are so scared part of the time that they are almost physically incapacitated, and yet they manage to carry out their duties in the cold and snow. As might be expected, the commissioned officers and the powers that run the American Army are not favorably presented, and there is quite a bit of foul language. The author does not omit revolting but natural physical details. Before shipping out from the United States, four of the group got a weekend pass and tried to find a girl who would have sex with all four. Some of them had never had the experience previously. This episode has an unusual twist to it and is handled well. The book is highly recommended by young adult librarians.

The book could be used as a booktalk for an audience of boys. A few sentences from this note will give a little background and show that the Germans seem friendly. Then tell about the Christmas tree the Germans set up on the road and the Christmas gifts that are exchanged, pages 164–75.

A truly excellent account of the opening attack by the British on D-Day is *Pegasus Bridge, June 6, 1944.* In it Stephen Ambrose describes the training of D-Company of the Oxfordshire and Buckinghamshire Light Infantry by Major John Howard for glider landings in France and the capture of two very important bridges. He also depicts the taking of the bridges and the action for several days thereafter.

Wheeler, Richard S.

Winter Grass.   1983.   Walker.

In 1881 John Quincy Putnam trades two steers for a little white girl whom a band of Piegans have with them. The child and her parents had been traveling by wagon westward when they were attacked by Indians. The adults had been killed, but the Indians had carried off the child. She had been passed from one band to another until Quin saw her. He had lost his own family in a tragedy before he came west, so he is alone except for the men who work for him. Eventually Missy, as Quin calls her, overcomes her fear, and they establish a good father-daughter relationship. Quin is a forward-looking rancher who tries out new ideas about cattle raising and caring for the land. He irks other ranchers by fencing part of his property in order to keep his special grasses for his own herd. The story opens in 1886, when there has been no rain for some time. The grass does not grow during the drought, and neighbors cut the wire so that their herds can get at the grass on Quin's ranch. This is not Quin's only problem. A detective has traced Missy's relatives, who may want to take the girl away from him. Quin's attorney in town is Nicole Aimont, a young woman carrying on her father's law office. She is in love with Quin, but there is a twenty-year difference in their ages, and Quin thinks she would never consider him eligible. Although at times things seem to go against him, he keeps finding ways to come out a little ahead. The winter of 1887 is one of the worst anyone has experienced, and Quin and Missy are housebound for many weeks. Most of the herds die that winter, and some of the ranchers have to give up and return east. But Quin has boarded out some of the best cattle, and he has a nucleus with which to begin again in the spring. Eventually the remaining ranchers realize that Quin's ideas about improving the quality of his stock and the grass are right and should be copied. At the end of the book he is able to adopt Missy, and Nicole decides she will marry him.

"You can't keep a good man down" is certainly the theme of this story, and the reader rejoices in Quin's success. Wheeler has done well in depicting his major characters, and the story holds the reader's interest.

The episode in which Quin acquires Missy and learns her story could be used in a booktalk, pages 12–15.

Also suggest *Sitka* by Louis L'Amour. Left an orphan at an early age, Jean LaBarge survives by trapping and gathering herbs in the treacherous Great Swamp. When he saves Captain Hutchins's life, the man takes him along on a trip west. This experience in trading and trapping gives Jean the experience he needs in Alaska, which then belongs to the Russians. His life is full of adventure, conflict, and narrow escapes. In *Thirsty*, Andrew Dequasie tells of Grandpa, who once lived in the small Idaho gold-mining town called Thirsty. He has told his young grandson many stories about the town so often that the boy knows them by heart. One day the two of them visit Thirsty. Realizing that the old man is lost in his memories, the lad sits down on the edge of the porch of the old Thirsty saloon and recalls the stories.

Whitnell, Barbara

The Ring of Bells. 1982. Coward, McCann.

Jenny's mother had left home when her parents disapproved of her marriage to a young actor. As the story opens, Jenny's father has deserted them years earlier and her mother has been struggling to support them. She becomes seriously ill and dies when Jenny is about fifteen. Her grandfather takes Jenny home with him to Collingford, where he and grandmother operate an inn, the Ring of Bells. Jenny is a good worker and before long is learning how to prepare the fine meals that the inn serves. Jenny falls in love with the oldest son of the Leyton family, who lives on a very large farm nearby. Although Jenny is lower in social rank than the Leytons, Roger wants to marry her. Her grandmother dies of a stroke, probably brought on by her rage at Jenny's proposed marriage. Roger decides to give up his title to the farm, Priors, and buy the inn, in which Jenny's grandfather has now lost interest. Roger modernizes the inn, and Jenny works with him, doing most of the cooking. As business prospers, Roger buys other inns and also a lovely old house for the family they now have. For a while Jenny is concerned chiefly with the new home and children—until she realizes that she and Roger are growing apart. It doesn't take her long to change that situation. Their oldest daughter, Ellie, finishes at Oxford; the second daughter, Lucy, not interested in education, marries early and begins a family; and the oldest boy, Ben, quits school to enlist at the beginning of World War I. After the war Roger and the youngest son, Philip, decide to build the inn of their dreams, and Roger mortgages everything to pay for its construction. Things look bad for a while, but they weather the crisis with the aid of a cousin in America who routes some of his travel-bureau tours through their town. At the end of the story, as World War II breaks out, Roger and Jenny celebrate their golden wedding anniversary.

This is a long, detailed story of the ups and downs of a big family. Good judgment, patience, love, and enthusiasm help to solve the problems that arise. Characters are well drawn, and there are many that could not be mentioned above.

Immediately after Roger has told Jenny that he loves her, she meets his brother Mark, who tells her in no uncertain terms that she is not good enough to marry into the Leyton family, pages 71–73. Or use the scene with her grandmother, when the old lady tells Jenny that Roger will never marry her, pages 74–76.

Whitnell has also written *The Song of the Rainbird*, in which a young English girl in the early 1900s goes out to Africa to marry the young man she loves. When she arrives in Nairobi and learns he has been killed, she teaches school or stays with friends until after World War I, when she marries a soldier returned from the war. This is an interesting view of the white settlers in Africa. *All Their Kingdoms* by Madeleine Polland concerns a family in Ireland. Matthew and Celia O'Connor are a wealthy young couple with a country home and a lovely house in Dublin. When Owen, the oldest boy, is twelve, Matt catches a fever and dies, and Celia dies six years later. Celia's brother, who has control of the property and funds, takes the boys out of school and makes them labor on the farm. Owen escapes to the United States to try to earn enough money to open the country home and put the farm into production, but it is his son who carried out his father's dream. My girls liked the picture of Ireland and the well-drawn characters.

Wilkins, Roy, with *Tom Matthews*

Standing Fast: The Autobiography of Roy Wilkins.
1982.   Viking.

Roy Wilkins is a man any young person can admire and strive to emulate. His parents are the son and daughter of slaves and have to leave Mississippi in 1900 to avoid being lynched. They go to St. Louis, where their three children are born. Roy's mother dies in 1908, and Roy, his brother, and his sister are adopted by his mother's sister and her husband, Elizabeth and Sam Williams, who live in St. Paul, Minnesota. They are a fine couple who sacrifice to give the children advantages their parents could not have provided. Roy works his way through the University of Minnesota with his Uncle Sam's help. He becomes a member of the university newspaper staff and soon proves his ability as a reporter and night editor. This experience provides a job for him when he graduates. He becomes editor of the *St. Paul Appeal*, a black newspaper. He also joins the local branch of the NAACP and the Urban League; these memberships and his editorship bring introductions to black leaders who visit the city. Shortly, Wilkins is offered a news editor position with the *Kansas City Call*, a stronger, larger paper. While in Missouri, he meets a young woman who becomes his wife. In 1931 his good work leads to the position of assistant secretary and later secretary of the NAACP at its headquarters in New York City. Wilkins recalls, year by year, the fight for civil rights and the parts that various presidents and members of Congress played in promoting or deemphasizing equal opportunity for all citizens of the United States. He is very frank in placing the blame for the slow development of civil rights on the shoulders of white citizens, particularly in the South. He tells of the murders of black civil rights workers, of Robert Kennedy's death, and of Martin Luther King's. His story includes the many marches that blacks made in Washington, D.C., in order to emphasize their desire for equality. Each march was noted for its lack of violence.

Wilkins writes very well, and his narrative fires the interest of the reader at the very beginning. Many events caused him indignation over the years, but he never lost his equilibrium. When hot heads threatened to commit violent acts, he was often able to calm them down. At other times, when riots broke out across the country, he kept a firm hand on the helm of the NAACP, and the public did not turn against all black people. He was criticized at times for not doing more for the black cause, but he was wise enough to see into the future and steer a course that would gain more in the end. He pays tribute to many black people.

A booktalk can include the letter his mother writes to her sister when she knows her physical condition is growing much worse. The speaker can include Sam Williams's determination to keep the children together and tell about their first months in their new home, pages 21–25. Or the booktalker can use small episodes from Wilkins's university years, pages 41–48.

What Manner of Man by Lerone Bennett traces the development of Martin Luther King's philosophy of nonviolence. Admiration for King grows as the reader watches his growth as a national leader. Younger students may want to skip scattered sentences about Hegel's and Gandhi's ideas that fascinated King.

Wooley, Persia

Child of the Northern Spring. 1987. Poseidon.

King Leodegrance of Rheged, a kingdom in northern Britain, travels with his family about the kingdom during the year so that he can know and deal immediately with any problems of his people. Guinevere, the king's daughter, loves horses, can ride, and has spent many hours around the animals. When she is nine her mother demands that she learn to run a household and gain some competence in spinning, weaving, and needlework. That winter is long and difficult, and the royal household sacrifices in order to share with its subjects. The weather is bad, and many come down with fever and die. The queen and her little son are among them. Guinevere and her father survive, and when the weather improves, their retinue moves sadly on. A family of Irish refugees asks permission to settle in Rheged and gives two children as hostages to ensure that they will not double-cross their new neighbors. The Irish have often invaded Britain. Thus Guinevere acquires two of her dearest friends, Brigit and Kevin, both twelve years of age. Brigit is Christian, while Kevin and the people of Rheged are not. One day word comes that King Uther is dead and that Arthur Pendragon is his successor. Britain is divided into a number of small kingdoms whose kings sometimes fight each other if they are not fighting Irish or Saxon invaders. Not all these rulers welcome Arthur as High King, and he has to fight for the right to the title. He is successful, and when it comes time for him to choose a queen, he selects Guinevere, whom he had once seen briefly. He sends Merlin and Bedivere to bring her to him. The girl's hand has been sought by many, but she has spurned them all. She does not really want to marry Arthur, but she gives in to her father's wishes. Most of the story tells of her journey from Rheged to meet Arthur and of the development of their relationship as they travel to the capital before their marriage. Guinevere is an intelligent, observant girl, and she is able to make suggestions that Arthur accepts. For example, she has seen what an Arab boy could do on horseback because he had stirrups. The British did not know about these attachments. When Arthur wants to develop a troop of cavalry, she suggests that stirrups would make them much more efficient riders, and she is right.

Wooley alternates chapters about Guinevere's growing up years in the first part of the book with events on the long journey to meet Arthur. This book is the first of a trilogy that the author plans. It is a very well written, engrossing story. Because it is told from Guinevere's viewpoint, it is different from most King Arthur stories. The author's careful research adds a

150

great deal to the enjoyment of the book because it brings the reader closer to the characters and their activities.

Chapter 3 gives a good idea of what life is like for Guinevere as a child, when her parents travel with their retinue. In chapter 1 Guinevere plans to run away rather than marry Arthur. Her companion, Brigit, talks her out of it and suggests she tell her father in the morning how she feels. The reader learns why she accepts the proposed marriage.

Because the book is so new, I have not had the opportunity to gather teenage opinions about it. However, I am sure the girls will love it, as they did these following books, which they highly recommended. In *Hawk of May* Gillian Bradshaw tells of Gwalchmai, second son of King Lot MacCormac of Erin. He has a magic sword and is a great fighter, but Arthur refuses to allow him to join his knights for a long time because he suspects the lad is tied to the powers of Darkness. *Kingdom of Summer* continues Gwalchmai's story but with a new main character, Rhys, the son of a clansman farmer with holdings not far from Camlann. Rhys goes as a servant with Gwalchmai in search of Elidan, an aristocratic girl he has wronged. Rhys is eventually drawn into the conflict between Gwalchmai and his sorceress mother, Morgawse. In *Winter's Shadow* Arthur's queen, Gwynhwyfar, tells of the years of her marriage, when Arthur's illegitimate sons divide the knights by innuendo and the queen drifts into a love affair with Bedwyn, Arthur's war leader. This is a sad story that ends with most of the characters dead. Other authors of King Arthur stories are Mary Steward, Terence H. White, and Alan Jay Lerner.

Wortman, Elmo

Almost Too Late. 1981. Random House.

Elmo Wortman had been a carpenter until his health failed. He is also the divorced father of four: Margery, Cindy, Randy, and Jena. He and the children put their belongings into a sailboat they have built and finally reach Craig, Alaska, where the children can go to school. They live as much as possible on food gathered from beaches, tidelands, and waters. The nearest orthodontist is two or three days' travel away. On February 13, 1979, they motor out of the harbor after their dentist appointments. They run into bad weather, and eventually the boat breaks up and sinks near an unidentified island. Cindy, sixteen, and Jena, twelve, land near one another and take refuge right up the beach. The next morning Cindy finds Randy, and then they find their Dad. Randy has matches in a glass jar inside his floatcoat, and he and Cindy bring everything that washes up on the shore to where their Dad and Jena stay by the fire. One of the sails comes ashore, and that provides shelter, but almost no food is found. Dad finally decides where they are. On the far end of the next island there is an occupied cabin, but they need a raft to reach it. When the raft has been built, they set out, but they only make about two miles. They have gone six days without a meal. Weather holds them up for two days. They are wet all the time, but the floatcoats provide some warmth for their upper bodies. On the third day they cross to Dall Island but have to stay there several days because of high winds. When they arrive at the place where they think the cabin is just around the corner, Randy and Dad leave the girls sheltered under the sail, saying they will be back in three hours with help. However, they are wrong about their location, and it is two days before they reach the cabin, which is unoccupied but unlocked. There is plenty of food and firewood, and their frozen feet begin to thaw; it is impossible to walk or sleep because of the pain. As day after day passes, they are sure the girls have died. On March 10 they are able to go for the girls' bodies, but on reaching them, find the girls still alive. When they get back to the cabin, someone has been there and seen the note Dad left. He has gone for help, and soon a helicopter comes and carries the family to the hospital, where all recover.

Readers are quickly caught up in the story, reading breathlessly as they hope and pray these courageous people will survive and reach safety. It is quite incredible that they did, and their father gives his children the credit for his own survival. A well-done true story.

As the boat is sinking, they sit on the railing with their feet over the side, while Randy and Dave give instructions: "Grab the rocks and pull yourselves out." "Don't let the water drag you back." "Each one is on his own." "Be ready to go when I tell you." "Now!" Jena panics in the water. Pages 42–52 tell what happens to them before they reach land.

In *Survive the Savage Sea,* Dougal Robertson tells about his family of six, who are rescued after 38 days in a fiberglass dinghy after whales have attacked and sunk their schooner. Another story of shipwreck is *Adrift.* When his small sloop sinks west of the Canary Islands, Steven Callahan takes refuge in a 5½-foot inflated raft equipped with lots of gadgets but only a little food and water. It takes him 76 days of drifting across the Atlantic to reach an island in the Caribbean; meanwhile, he exists on raw fish and water distilled in two small stills. In *Staying Alive* Maurice Bailey describes the 117 days he and his wife spend in a 5-foot rubber dinghy and a small raft after their ketch has been sunk by a wounded whale.

Zelazny, Roger

Nine Princes in Amber. 1970. Doubleday.

In leg casts and multiple bandages, Corwin comes to in a hospital room, not knowing who he is or how he has gotten there, but sure that he has to get out as quickly as possible. After he uses a bit of strong-arm on the orderly and blackmail on the administrator, he is able to get away from the private sanitarium and go to New York to see his sister, whose name and address he has pressured the administrator into providing. By skillful questioning he learns a little about his identity. The next day his brother Random calls from California to ask for protection and says he is flying to New York that day. Meanwhile Corwin has discovered that he is from Amber, and when Random arrives, he offers to join Corwin against this brother, Eric, who is planning to be crowned king of Amber. They borrow Flora's Mercedes and start for Amber with Random guiding, going through numerous time warps. Occasionally even the car changes its form. Corwin cannot remember how this is done, although he knows he could once do it. When he finally admits that he has lost his memory, Random suggests Corwin go to Rebma, which is a reflection of Amber within the sea, and where he can walk the Pattern and regain his memory. Corwin describes the experience of walking the Pattern. As he walks, he recalls episodes from his life and decides that he first visited shadow Earth in the sixteenth century, having been a professional soldier from those years to the present. He learns that Amber is the greatest city, the only real city, that has ever been and ever will be. All other cities are but shadows, reflecting some phase of Amber. Having finished the difficult walk, he receives the power of the Pattern so that he can transfer himself to anywhere he wants to be. After a visit to Amber, where he is lucky to escape with his life, he joins his brother Bleys against Eric. They are completely defeated on land and sea, and Corwin is taken prisoner. After he is forced to watch Eric crowned, Corwin is blinded and thrown in a dungeon. At the end of three years, regeneration begins in his eye sockets, and by the time his eyes are restored, he has found a way to escape from Amber, still intent on somehow defeating Eric.

Young people are still enthusiastic about this fantasy and its sequels, feeling it is the best series they know. The books read like fairy stories with fantastic creatures, magic cards, fabulous powers of strength, body transference, and mind communication.

The descent into Rebma described in chapter 5 could be worked into a booktalk.

The natural follow-ups are the sequels, *Guns of Avalon, Sign of the Unicorn, The Hand of Oberon,* and *The Courts of Chaos.* The last book brings the big family back together with the exception of Brand, Deirdre, and their father Oberon, who have died. Random has been named king by the unicorn. Merlin, a son Corwin did not know existed, has joined them and will need a lot of Corwin's attention. In the making is a new series concerning Merlin. In *Darkover Landfall* Marion Zimmer Bradley describes the aftermath of the crash landing of a starship of an unknown world. It carries a crew, a large group of colonists bound for Coronis, and some scientists. When it proves impossible to repair the starship, the survivors have to try to establish a permanent colony. Fortunately the contraceptive the women used is no longer working, and there is a chance for reproduction to sustain the colony for a time. In *The Winds of Darkover* the colony is well established, and people come from and go to other worlds regularly. Dan Barron has worked for five years as a dispatcher at the spaceport. One night at a crucial moment his mind is taken over by a terrible hallucination, and catastrophe is averted only narrowly. Disgraced, he is transferred to a job in the mountainous interior. The hallucinations continue, and, finally, Dan's body is taken over by a desperate man trying to save his home and family.

After many strange events Dan finds himself better off than he had been when he first came to Darkover. Another series of stories that is very popular with some teenagers is the Lord of the Rings trilogy by J. R. R. Tolkien.

Subject Index of Main Entries

Adventure
Almost Too Late, 151
Aviator, 51
Bannister's Chart, 137
Hub, 75
Rainbow Chasers, 109
Shining Mountain, 4
Silent World, 28
Sinbad Voyage, 129
Tracking Marco Polo, 131
Twenty Thousand Leagues
    under the Sea, 138
Winter of the White Seal, 73

Animals
Cry of the Kalahari, 120
Dark Horse, 54
Matthew Ratton, 89
Most of My Patients Are
    Animals, 115
On Horses, 38
Rustle in the Grass, 68
Searching for Hidden Animals,
    110
Wake of the Storm, 27
Whale of the Victoria Cross, 6
Winter of the White Seal, 73

Aviation
Aviator, 51
Bright Blue Sky, 72
Into the Mouth of the Cat, 105

Ballet
Thursday's Children, 55

Biography and Autobiography
Anne Frank: The Diary of a
    Young Girl, 44
Anne Frank Remembered, 52
Home Is the Sailor, 59
Lovestrong, 61
Mary, 113
Mary Lou, 124
No Job for a Lady, 101
One of the Lucky Ones, 21
Profiles in Courage, 88
Rainbow Chasers, 109
Rookie, 57
Standing Fast, 148

Blind
Hunter in the Dark, 134
One of the Lucky Ones, 21

Boys
Bracken, 140
Great Expectations, 34
Hard on the Wind, 80
Hub, 75
Nima: A Sherpa in Connecticut,
    46
Peace Breaks Out, 91
They Cage the Animals at
    Night, 15
Thursday's Children, 55

Chinese
Gates of Grace, 20
Little Sister, 49
One of the Lucky Ones, 21
Tea with the Black Dragon, 104

Civil Rights
Black like Me, 63
Standing Fast, 148
To Kill a Mockingbird, 98

Civil War
Elkhorn Tavern, 84
Red Badge of Courage, 31

Classics
And Then There Were None, 23
Complete Sherlock Holmes, 36
Great Expectations, 34
Jane Eyre, 12
Red Badge of Courage, 31
Twenty Thousand Leagues
    under the Sea, 138
War of the Worlds, 142

Courage
Allegiance, 60
Almost Too Late, 151
Aviator, 51
Cry of the Kalahari, 120
Devil Boats, 11
Girl of the Sea of Cortez, 3
Into the Mouth of the Cat, 105
One of the Lucky Ones, 21
Profiles in Courage, 88
Red Badge of Courage, 31
Run, Patty, Run, 30
Shining Mountain, 4
Tracking Marco Polo, 131
Winter of the White Seal, 73

Danger
Almost Too Late, 151
Bullet Train, 123
Day We Bombed Utah, 47
Devil Boats, 11
Fate of the Earth, 128
Girl of the Sea of Cortez, 3
Shining Mountain, 4

Death
Bracken, 140

Disaster
Cold Sea Rising, 117
Day We Bombed Utah, 47
Fate of the Earth, 128
Hiero's Journey, 96
Hiroshima, 76
Julie, 112
Night to Remember, 99

Family Life
Almost Too Late, 151
Brandywine, 126
Girl of the Sea of Cortez, 3
Home Is the Sailor, 59
Julie, 112
Little Sister, 49
Patchwork Clan, 103
Rainbow Chasers, 109
Ring of Bells, 146
Run, Patty, Run, 30
Thursday's Children, 55
To Kill a Mockingbird, 98

Fantasy
House between the Worlds, 7
Lost Tale, 40
Nine Princes in Amber, 153
Portrait of Jennie, 119
Quest for the Faradawn, 41
Rustle in the Grass, 68
Child of the Northern Spring,
    149
Tea with the Black Dragon, 104

Future
Fate of the Earth, 128
Make Room! Make Room!, 65

Generation Gap
Bracken, 140
Hub, 75

Girls
Anne Frank: The Diary of a
    Young Girl, 44
Aviator, 51

Beacon at Alexandria, 9
Girl of the Sea of Cortez, 3
Julie, 112
Little Sister, 49
Mary Lou, 124
One of the Lucky Ones, 21
Run, Patty, Run, 30
Thursday's Children, 55

Handicapped
Aviator, 51
Hunter in the Dark, 134
No Language but a Cry, 33
One Child, 70
One of the Lucky Ones, 21
Run, Patty, Run, 30
Turnabout Children, 107

History
Clan of the Cave Bear, 1
Beacon at Alexandria, 9
Brandywine, 126
Bright Blue Sky, 72
Elkhorn Tavern, 84
Longsword, 136
Killdeer Mountain, 14
Profiles in Courage, 88
Rainbow Chasers, 109
Red Badge of Courage, 31
Season of the Yellow Leaf,
     86

Horses
Dark Horse, 54
On Horses, 38

Human Interest
Bracken, 140
Nima: A Sherpa in Connecticut,
     46
No Language but a Cry, 33
One Child, 70
Turnabout Children, 107

Humor or Satire
Little Sister, 49
Most of My Patients Are
     Animals, 115
Whale of the Victoria Cross, 6

International Intrigue
Day of Judgment, 78

Love Stories
Child of the Northern Spring,
     149
Jane Eyre, 12
Longsword, 136
Portrait of Jennie, 119
Rebecca, 37
Ring of Bells, 146
Wake of the Storm, 27

Marriage
Cry of the Kalahari, 120
Home Is the Sailor, 59
Lovestrong, 61

Masquerade
Beacon at Alexandria, 9

Minorities
     BLACK
Black like Me, 63
Mary, 113
Rookie, 57
Standing Fast, 148
To Kill a Mockingbird, 98
     INDIAN
Season of the Yellow Leaf, 86
     JEWISH
Anne Frank: The Diary of a
     Young Girl, 44
Anne Frank Remembered, 52
Return to Auschwitz, 66

Mystery
And Then There Were None, 23
Bannister's Chart, 137
Complete Sherlock Holmes, 36
Danger, 43
Dead on Arrival, 132
Hanging Tree, 93
Hunter in the Dark, 134
Rebecca, 37

Pioneers
Killdeer Mountain, 14
Rainbow Chasers, 109

Precocious Young People
Bracken, 140
Ender's Game, 18
Mary, 113
One of the Lucky Ones, 21

Science
Cry of the Kalahari, 120
Lucy: The Beginning of
     Humankind, 82
Searching for Hidden Animals,
     110
Silent World, 28

Science Fiction
Ender's Game, 18
Hiero's Journey, 96
House between the Worlds, 7
Kindred, 17
Make Room! Make Room!, 65
Nine Princes in Amber, 153
Twenty Thousand Leagues
     under the Sea, 138
2010: Odyssey Two, 25
War of the Worlds, 142

Sea
Almost Too Late, 151
Bannister's Chart, 137
Cold Sea Rising, 117
Girl of the Sea of Cortez, 3
Hard on the Wind, 80
Night to Remember, 99
Silent World, 28
Sinbad Voyage, 129
Twenty Thousand Leagues
     under the Sea, 138
Whale of the Victoria Cross, 6

Sex
Love and Sex in Plain Language,
     83

Social Problems
No Language but a Cry, 33
One Child, 70
They Cage the Animals at
     Night, 15
Turnabout Children, 107

The South
Black like Me, 63
Kindred, 17
Mary, 113
To Kill a Mockingbird, 98

Sports
Mary Lou, 124
Rookie, 57
Run, Patty, Run, 30
Shining Mountain, 4

Suspence
Allegiance, 60
Almost Too Late, 151
Aviator, 51
Beacon at Alexandria, 9
Bullet Train, 123
Cold Sea Rising, 117
War of the Worlds, 142

Teens
Almost Too Late, 151
Anne Frank: The Diary of a
     Young Girl, 44
Anne Frank Remembered, 52
Girl of the Sea of Cortez, 3
Hard on the Wind, 80
Julie, 112
Mary Lou, 124
Nima: A Sherpa in Connecticut,
     46
Peace Breaks Out, 91
Run, Patty, Run, 30

Terrorists
Bullet Train, 123

Travel
Almost Too Late, 151
Bannister's Chart, 137
Bill Kurtis on Assignment, 94
Sinbad Voyage, 129
Tracking Marco Polo, 131

Vietnam
Into the Mouth of the Cat, 105

Vocations
  ANTHROPOLOGIST
Lucy: The Beginning of
  Humankind, 82
  BALLET DANCER
Thursday's Children, 55
  DIVER
Silent World, 28
  DOCTOR
Lovestrong, 61
  HORSE TRAINER
On Horses, 38
  PILOT
Bright Blue Sky, 72
  PSYCHOLOGIST OR
    PSYCHOANALYST
No Language but a Cry, 33
One Child, 70
Turnabout Children, 107
  REPORTER
Bill Kurtis on Assignment, 94
  SCIENTISTS
Cry of the Kalahari, 120
  TEACHER
One Child, 70
Turnabout Children, 107
  VETERINARIAN
Most of My Patients Are
  Animals, 115

No Job for a Lady, 101
  ZOOLOGIST
Searching for Hidden Animals,
  110

Western
Killdeer Mountain, 14
Rainbow Chasers, 109
Winter Grass, 145

Women's Rights
Beacon at Alexandria, 9
No Job for a Lady, 101

World War I
Bright Blue Sky, 72

World War II
Allegiance, 60
Devil Boats, 11
Hiroshima, 76
Lost Tale, 40
Midnight Clear, 143
Return to Auschwitz, 66

Title Index

The books which are fully annotated are indicated by an aster-isk (°) in front of the page number on which the complete annotation begins.

Abandon Ship, 101
A.B.C. Murders, 24
Adrift, 153
Adventures and Memoirs, 36
Aka, 4
All My Patients Are under the Bed, 117
All Their Kingdoms, 148
Allegiance, °60
Almost Too Late, °151
Amindra Gamble, 12
And I Alone Survived, 52
And Then There Were None, °23, 37
Animals Come First, 117
Anne Frank: A Portrait in Courage, 45
Anne Frank Remembered 46, °52
Anne Frank: The Diary of a Young Girl, °44, 53
April Morning, 32
Ark on the Flood, 112
Around the World Submerged, 140
Artful Dodger, 58
Ascent to Civilization, 83
Assignment: Wildlife, 102
Aviator, °51

Ballet Life behind the Scenes, 57
Banker, 44
Bannister's Chart, °137
Barbara Jordan: A Self-portrait, 115
Barefoot Brigade, 85
Basketball My Way, 125
Beacon at Alexandria, °9
Beyond Reach: The Search for the Titanic, 100
Bill Kurtis on Assignment, 48, °94
Black like Me, °63, 99
Bloodtide, 94
Blue Savage, 88
Body in the Library, 24
Bowfin, 12
Bracken, °140
Brandywine, °126
Brendan Voyage, 130
Bright Blue Sky, °72
Bullet Train, °123

Call the Darkness Down, 41
Camera Never Blinks, 95
Case Book, 36
Case of the Poisoned Eclairs, 135

Case of the Sliding Pool, 135
Cave of the Moving Shadows, 2
Challenge, 6
Challenging Heights, 73
Child of the Northern Spring, °149
Childhood, 68
Chinese Bell Murders, 105
Chrissie: My Own Story, 125
Christy, 113
Circle of Children, 34
City Kid, 71, 108
Clan of the Cave Bear, °1
Cloak of Darkness, 79
Cold and the Dark, 98, 128
Cold Sea Rising, °117
Combat Crew, 73
Coming of Age in Mississippi, 64, 99
Company of Swans, 56
Complete Sherlock Holmes, °36
Cosmos, 26
Courts of Chaos, 154
Crossfire Killings, 94
Cruelest Night, 12
Cry of the Kalahari, 63, °120
Cry of the Seals, 75

Dancers of Sycamore Street, 56
Dancing for Balanchine, 57
Danger, °43
Dark Horse, °54
Dark Quartet, 13
Darkness and the Dawn, 10
Darkover Landfall, 154
David Copperfield, 35
Day of Judgment, °78
Day One: Before Hiroshima and After, 78, 128
Day We Bombed Utah, °47
Dead on Arrival, °132
Death in the Greenhouse, 94
Death of an Expert Witness, 94
Deep Range, 140
Deliverance at Los Baños, 61
Devil Boats: The PT War against Japan, °11

Different Drum, 34
Distant Summer, 41
Dolphins, 4
Dove, 59, 81
Dr. Wildlife, 117
Dragon and the George, 9
Dragonwings, 21

Earthchild, 19
Eiger: Wall of Death, 6
Elk-dog Heritage, 88
Elkhorn Tavern, °84
Emergence, 20
Ender's Game, °18
Enola Gay, 77
Escape from Laos, 107
Evil under the Sun, 24
Exploring Underwater, 4

Family of Eagles, 28
Fate of the Earth, 98, °128
Field of Buttercups, 45
Find a Safe Place, 16
First Men on the Moon, 143
Flight of the Condor, 96
Flying Flynns, 62
Flying Free, 28
For the World to See, 102
Fragments of Isabella, 68

Gates of Grace, °20, 127
Geri, 31
Giants in the Earth, 110
Girl of the Sea of Cortez, °3
Gizelle, Save the Children, 68
Gone the Dreams and Dancing, 87
Good Night, Mr. Tom, 141
Grand Tour: A Traveler's Guide to the Solar System, 26
Great Expectations, 17, °34
Green Mansions, 120
Guns of Avalon, 154

Hacey Miller, 32
Hand of Oberon, 154
Handful of Stars, 31
Hanging Tree, °93

Hanna and Walter: A Love Story, 68
Hard on the Wind, °80
Hawk of May, 151
Hidden Target, 80
Hidden Wrath, 135
Hiding Place, 53
Hiero's Journey, °96
Hiroshima, °76
His Last Bow, °36
Hitchhiker's Guide to the Galaxy, 26
Home Is the Sailor, °59
Homesick, My Own Story, 50
Horse to Remember, 55
Hound of the Baskervilles, 36
House between the Worlds, °7
Hub, °75
Hunter in the Dark, °134

I Am One of You Forever, 76
I Hear Them Calling My Name, 64
If We Could Hear the Grass Grow, 71
Imperial Earth, 143
In the Eye of the Typhoon, 50
In the Frame, 44
In Winter's Shadow, 151
International Velvet, 55
Into the Mouth of the Cat, °105
Invisible Walls, 68
Inyo-Sierra Passage, 52

Jane Eyre, °12, 38
Jason Voyage, 130
Johnny Logan, Shawnee Spy, 87
Joy in the Morning, 60
Judgment in St. Peter's, 80
Julie, °112

Kerry: Agent Orange and an American Family, 48
Killdeer Mountain, °14
Killing in Antiques, 94
Kindred, °17
Kingdom of Summer, 151
Kurt Thomas on Gymnastics, 58

Lady of Rhuddesmere, 137
Laska, 91
Last Day of Creation, 18
Last Days of Pompeii, 10
Last Moments of a World, 50
Leap Year, 57
Lena, 115
Lest Innocent Blood Be Shed, 53
Lion's Share, 122
Listening Silence, 41
Little Sister, °49
Live Bait, 94
Living Sea, 29
London Season, 13
Longsword, °136
Lord God Made Them All, 116
Lord of the Rings, 154
Lost Tale, °40
Lottery Rose, 15
Love and Sex in Plain Language, °83
Lovestrong, °61
Lovey, a Very Special Child, 34, 108
Lucy: The Beginning of Humankind, 2, °82
Lurcher, 91

Make Room! Make Room!, °65
Making of a Woman Vet, 117
Man: 1200 Years under the Sea, 29
Man Who Rode the Sharks, 4
Many a Voyage, 89
Marathon Miranda, 31
Marco Polo, Venetian Adventurer, 132
Marva Collins' Way, 115
Mary, 64, °113
Mary Lou, °124
Massacre at Salt Creek, 15
Matter of Risk, 29, 140
Matthew Ratton, °89
Maxwell's Train, 124
Mayday! Mayday!, 51
Member of the Wedding, 99
Midnight Clear, °143
Mike King Story, 31

Millenium, 143
Missing Links, 2
Morro Castle, 100
Most of My Patients Are
    Animals, °115
Mr. and Mrs. Bo Jo Jones, 60
Murder Most Irregular, 37
Murder on the Orient Express,
    24
Murphy's Boy, 71
My Animal Kingdom, One by
    One, 117
My Cousin Rachel, 38
My Wild World, 39, 117
Myself When Young, 38
Mysterious Island, 140

Neanderthals, 2
Neverending Story, 42
Night Lives On, 100
Night She Died, 133
Night to Remember, °99
Nima: A Sherpa in Connecticut,
    °46
Nine Princes in Amber, 153
19 Steps up the Mountain, 104
No High Ground, 77
No Job for a Lady, 40, °101
No Language but a Cry, °33
No Room for Man, 66
Nop's Trials, 91

Old Man and the Boy, 141
Oliver Twist, 35
On Horses, °38, 55
On the Road with Charles
    Kuralt, 96
Once More the Hawks, 73
One Child, °70
One Goal, 58
One Life, 83
One of the Lucky Ones, °21, 50
Operation White Lion, 122
Out of the Silent Planet, 143

Passing Shots, 126
Patchwork Clan, °103
Path to a Silent Country, 13
Peace Breaks Out, °91

Pegasus Bridge, June 6, 1944,
    145
Perilous Seas, 101
Phantom over Vietnam, 107
Poisoned Web, 135
Portrait of Jennie, °119
Postman, 98
Prince of Whales, 7
Profiles in Courage, °88
Proof, 44
Puppet for a Corpse, 133

Quest for the Faradawn, °41, 70
Quo Vadis, 10

Rainbow Chasers, °109
Raspberry One, 107
Rebecca, 13, °37
Red Badge of Courage, °31
Red Fox, 80
Reflex, 44
Rest in Pieces, 134
Return to Auschwitz, °66
Reunion, 92
Righteous Gentile, 53
Ring of Bells, °146
Roman, 86
Rookie, °57
Rosey: The Gentle Giant, 58
Ruffles on My Longjohns, 63,
    110
Run, Patty, Run, °30
Running Wild, 138
Rustle in the Grass, °68

Sacrament, 52
Sailor's War, 12
Savage Arena, 5
Saved! The Story of the Andrea
    Doria, 100
Seal Woman, 120
Search for the Past, 83
Searching for Hidden Animals,
    °110
Season of the Yellow Leaf, °86
Second Daughter, 23, 50
Secret Languages of the Sea, 4,
    111
Sentinel, 26

79 Squares, 141
Shawno, 91
Sherlock Bones, 117
Sherlock Holmes and the Case
    of the Raleigh Legacy, 37
Shine of Rainbows, 16
Shining Mountain, °4
Ship Must Die, 12
Sign of the Four, 36
Sign of the Unicorn, 154
Silent World, °28, 140
Sinbad Voyage, °129
Singletusk, 2
Sitka, 146
Six Feet Under, 134
Six Letter Word for Death,
    134
So Remorseless a Havoc, 7
Sole Survivor, 101
Some of My Best Friends Are
    Animals, 28
Some Survived, 61
Song of the Kingdom, 43
Song of the Meadowlark, 88
Song of the Rainbird, 147
Sounding, 7
Special Deliverance, 18
Special Kind of Courage, 89
Spring Came on Forever, 127
Square of Sky, 45
Standing Fast, °148
State of Emergency, 119
State of Stony Lonesome, 113
Staying Alive, 153
Still River, 20
Students against Tyranny, 53
Study in Scarlet, 36
Survive the Savage Sea, 153
Susquehanna, 127

Tailchaser's Song, 70
Tale of Two Cities, 35
Tea with the Black Dragon,
    °104
They Accepted the Challenge,
    31
They Cage the Animals at
    Night, °15
Thirsty, 146

30 Centuries under the Sea, 29
Thistle & Co., 28
Thursday's Children, °55
Tiger of the Snows, 6
Time after Time, 18
Time Machine, 18
Time of the Dark, 8
Time of the Fourth Horseman,
    66
To Fly a Kite, 142
To Kill a Mockingbird, °98
Tony: Our Journey Together,
    104, 141
Tracking Marco Polo, °131
Travels of Marco Polo, 132
Turnabout Children, °107
Twenty Thousand Leagues
    under the Sea, °138
2061: Odyssey Three, 26
2010: Odyssey Two, °25

U-Boat Commander, 12
Unforsaken Hiero, 97
Unicorns in the Rain, 66
Uninvited Visitors, 143
Upstairs Room, 45

Valley of Fear, 36
Vedi, 23
Violent Face of Nature, 119

Waiting for an Army to Die,
    48
Wake of the Storm, °27
Walls: Resisting the Third
    Reich, 54, 68
War of the Worlds, °142
Watership Down, 70
Wavecrest, 94
Way Station, 9, 143
Way to Fort Pillow, 32
Way West, 15
Whale of the Victoria Cross, 4,
    °6
What Manner of Man, 149
What's Happening to My Body?
    A Growing Up Guide for
    Girls and Their Mothers,
    84

What's Happening to My
    Body? Book for Boys, 84
White Lions of Timbavati, 122
White Shaman, 75
Wind from Hastings, 137
Winds of Darkover, 154
Winning Women, 125
Winter Grass, °145
Winter of the White Seal, °73
Winter's Shadow, 151
Woman of the People, 87
Woman Who Loved Reindeer, 42
Women and Wilderness, 102

Women at War, 68
Women in War, 102
Woodswoman, 102
Work of Her Hands, 102
Worlds Apart, 56
World's Apart, 132
Wuthering Heights, 13, 38

You May Plow Here, 115
You, Me, and a Few Billion
    More, 66

Zed, 124